THE JEWELRY ENGRAVERS MANUAL

R. Allen Hardy and John J. Bowman

Illustrations by R. Allen Hardy

DOVER PUBLICATIONS
Garden City, New York

Copyright

Bibliographical Note

The Dover edition, first published in 1994, is an unabridged
and unaltered republication of the revised edition of the work as
published by Van Nostrand Reinhold Company, New York, in
1976 (original edition, 1954).

Library of Congress Cataloging-in-Publication Data

Hardy R. Allen (Richard Allen)
 The jewelry engravers manual / R. Allen Hardy and John J.
Bowman.
  p.   cm.
 Reprint. Originally published: New York : Van Nostrand
Reinhold, 1976.
 Includes index.
 ISBN-13: 978-0-486-28154-4
 ISBN-10: 0-486-28154-X
 1. Jewelry   engraving.   2. Lettering.   3. Mono-
grams.   I. Bowman, John J.   II. Title.
TS729.H34   1994
739.27′5—dc20   94–1625
                                                      CIP

Manufactured in the United States of America
28154017
www.doverpublications.com

Preface

COMPARING THIS BOOK with the generality of books that are now on the market on the subject of engraving, the reader will see an important difference. Most of the current books on engraving are collections of designs for lettering, monograms, and units of decorative work, showing the forms and appearance of finished work, but *without adequate instructions on how to do the work* with cutting tools and other equipment; so that the books in question are helpful only to persons who have already acquired competent skill in the use of the tools with which the engraver must execute his work. But this jewelry engraving book is a comprehensive practical manual, written by a teacher of long experience in training pupils who have achieved outstanding success as artistic engravers; and it therefore supplies that technical knowledge which is the basis of well-developed skill with tools, without which the finest artistic designing is useless. In other words, this is a "how to do" book.

The instruction given is systematic, a guide to self-development that puts first things first, and explains step-by-step what to do and how to do it, in order to arrive eventually at competent ability in engraving. In its scope, the book covers initials and inscriptions in various alphabets, combinations of initials in monograms, and certain forms for the decoration and embellishment of engraved work, on the metals and other substances of which so many articles of utility and beauty are made.

While it is true that personal instruction in a good technical school, or by a competent individual teacher otherwise, is best of all for the mastery of an art, we believe that for the many who are unable to arrange for such instruction, this book comes nearest to it; and not only for learning how to engrave from the beginning, but we believe also that the book can be very helpful to many engravers

now engaged in this work vocationally, as a guide in making worth-
while improvement in their ability.

The instructions in this book are based upon a comprehensive
program of work to be done, the entirety of the program being di-
vided into eleven sections, designated by letters A to K inclusively.
These sections of the work-outline are printed separately at places
throughout the book, positioned wherever convenient for referring
to them, in relation to various subject-matter in the text.

In each of the sections, the work to be accomplished has two
aspects: first, learning to draw, with a lead-pencil on paper, the
elements of the designs and the complete designs later to be engraved, and then drawing these designs on surfaces of articles to be
engraved; and second, learning the use of various tools for cutting
the engraving. An all-important part of the latter work is the shaping and maintenance of the cutting tools in good condition for efficient work. Therefore the beginning of Chapter 1 deals with the
correct shaping and sharpening of square script gravers. The engraver needs many different kinds of these cutting tools or "gravers,"
all of them being variations on the basic type tool, which is the
square script graver.

Contents

THE JEWELRY
ENGRAVERS
MANUAL

Chapter 1

Correct Shaping and Sharpening of Square Script Gravers

BEFORE STARTING work on the program, the principal tools involved in the first steps will be described. In Fig. 1 is shown a square script graver and its handle which is of the adjustable type. The graver is clamped into the handle by the split metal ferrule near the front end of the handle, making the total length adjustable to suit large

FIG. 1. Square script graver and handle.

or smaller hands, and to maintain this length as the graver is gradually shortened by regrinding. The graver has a straight end, used on work of flat or convex-curved surfaces, and a bent end, for use on the inside of concave work, such as the inside of watch-case caps, cups, spoon-bowls, etc.

Gravers as manufactured and sold by tool dealers are not ready for use and must be ground to very definite forms and polished to

keen-cutting edges, in a variety of forms to be correct for the many different kinds of "cuts" that are required in the art. The mechanical device used for obtaining flat faces in grinding gravers is shown in Fig. 2. Its use will be explained fully in the proper place. Grinding and

FIG. 2. Graver holder for sharpening.

sharpening gravers is done on flat-faced slabs of abrasive material, either of natural stone or bonded synthetic grains; the latter mostly sold under the manufacturers' trade-marks "India oilstone" and "Carborundum," for quickly grinding to form. The "hard Arkansas" quarried natural stone is always used for the next step in sharpening. These stones may be bought with the two kinds mounted in pairs in a hinged wooden case as in Fig. 2, or each in a separate case. The other of the principal items of equipment needed for engraving is an engraving block, Fig. 3, which is a holder for all kinds of work. It is a mechanical turntable, its heavy iron ball-base resting in the doughnut-shaped, sand-filled leather pad on the bench. The two jaws on the revolving table are adjustable toward each other and the holes in the jaw-tops are

FIG. 3. Engraving holder and attachments.

used to hold the attachments shown in the box to the right of the block. With these attachments, almost any form of work can be held and the jaws tightened on it so that the work can be turned by one hand resting on the revolving table while the other hand manipulates the graver.

Now let us start work, following the steps listed at the front of the chapter.

1. Use of Mechanical Device

When sharpening a graver, the foot of the graver sharpener slides back and forth over a section of plate glass. The position of the glass section is most satisfactory when used as shown in Fig. 2. It can, however, be placed on top of the open part of the oilstone case, providing the hinge joints do not interfere by tilting the glass off level.

The graver sharpener (Fig. 2) enables the engraver to obtain mechanically accurate faces. The construction and theoretical operation of the graver sharpener is simple but actual manipulation requires a close study of technique. See Figs. 4, 5, 6, and 7. Here we see the faces presented to the stone in various ways to obtain desired conditions or results. Adjustments made to the graver sharpener in relation to the position of the graver with the stone, determine the accuracy of these faces.

The graver sharpener shown in Fig. 2 has three wing-nuts. One controls the adjustment of the belly angle; one controls the position or shape of the various faces; the other wing-nut serves to hold the graver firmly. With only two real adjustments to consider, sharpening the graver appears to be less of a problem than it really is. If the reader will keep it clear in his mind that the adjustments are made while holding the sharpener bottom upward, and the actual stoning is done with the position inverted (Fig. 2) no confusion will arise.

The cutting points of square script gravers have three faces. The two faces on the bottom or underside will be referred to as "the belly"; the one face on the top of the graver will be referred to as "the face." When sharpening, the steel graver is removed from the handle and placed in position in the graver sharpener.

To face either side of the belly (Fig. 4 and Fig. 5), first place the graver securely in the sharpener by tightening the wing-nut governing this adjustment. The next step is to line up the graver parallel or flat with the India stone. Since this type of graver is actually square and the slot in the sharpener forms a right angle, it is comparatively easy to position one side flat with the stone and the other

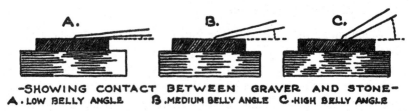

-SHOWING CONTACT BETWEEN GRAVER AND STONE-
A . LOW BELLY ANGLE   B .MEDIUM BELLY ANGLE   C .HIGH BELLY ANGLE

FIG. 4.

side perpendicular to it. If a straight-faced belly is desired, the sharpener may be set in this position by tightening the wing-nut governing this adjustment. If a slant-faced belly is wanted, the vertical side of the graver may be tilted slightly away from its upright position, depending on the direction of the slant desired.

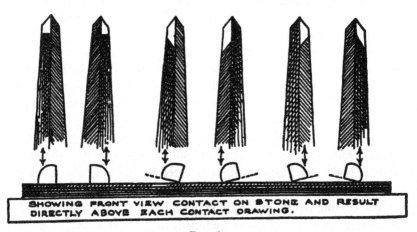

SHOWING FRONT VIEW CONTACT ON STONE AND RESULT
DIRECTLY ABOVE EACH CONTACT DRAWING.

FIG. 5

To tilt the graver, notice the right-angle slot in the sharpener. This will serve as a guide. Also, most sharpeners are marked with graduations, and the amount of tilt may be controlled accurately.

The next step is deciding on the amount of belly angle and setting the sharpener accordingly. For beginners, belly angles should best be on the low side. Average belly angles will fall between 8° and

SHARPENING THE FACE

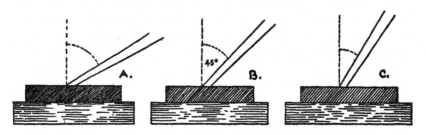

– SHOWING CONTACT BETWEEN GRAVER AND STONE –

A. LOW FACE ANGLE WEAKENS POINT B. CORRECT FACE ANGLE 45 DEGREES C. HIGH FACE ANGLE STRENGTHENS POINT.

FIG. 6.

12°. To set the angle, loosen the wing-nut governing this adjustment; allow the graver to lie flat on the India stone; raise the end attached to the sharpener slightly, and tighten the wing-nut. Exact

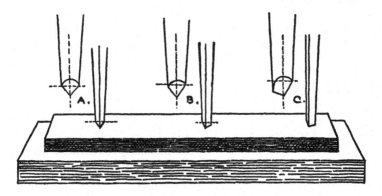

– SHOWING CONTACT FOR SHAPING FACE –

A. STRAIGHT FACE, GOOD FOR HAIRLINES. B. CUTTING EDGE BROUGHT FORWARD SLIGHTLY. IDEAL SHAPE FOR AVERAGE WORK. C. CUTTING EDGE TOO FAR FORWARD. AVOID THIS.

FIG. 7.

belly angles may be measured by using an ordinary geometric protractor.

Sharpening "the face" of the graver is a less complicated job. See Fig. 6 and Fig. 7. A 45° face angle is what is wanted for all beginning work, shown in Fig. 6B. Figures 7A, B, and C show three conditions; A and B being acceptable shapes and C indicating a shape to avoid. Since the student is interested solely in an average graver at this point, a combination of Fig. 6B and Fig. 7B is the shape and face angle wanted.

2. Stoning Belly and Face

Before using either stone, saturate them with oil. This may be done by pouring and spreading on a little oil at a time, allowing it to soak into the stone, and repeating the procedure until the stone will absorb no more. Oil, especially prepared for oilstones, may be bought from any dealer in jewelers' supplies, or the automobile motor oil sold as "Grade SAE 10," may be used.

The India stone is used to "rough out" or grind the faces. The Arkansas stone is used to "smooth out" or polish away the coarse lines remaining from the India stone. Emery paper is the final polishing agent, and should be used in grit 4-0.

After grinding a face, using the India stone, it should be immediately presented to the Arkansas stone, no further adjustment to the graver sharpener being necessary. Care must be taken to level up the stones so that no change results when turned over from one side to the other. The three faces are ground on the two stones first. When all three are complete, the graver is placed in the handle and polished by hand on 4-0 emery paper placed on top of a flat piece

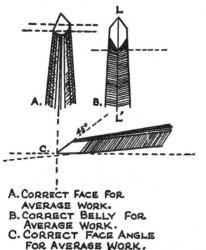

A. CORRECT FACE FOR AVERAGE WORK.
B. CORRECT BELLY FOR AVERAGE WORK.
C. CORRECT FACE ANGLE FOR AVERAGE WORK.

FIG. 8.

of glass (Fig. 13). Fig. 8 shows a graver sharpened for average work. The belly is always sharpened first and the two sides must meet at a point as in Fig. 8B. The same amount of metal is ground away on both sides so that the line of centers (L-L′) is not disturbed. If more is ground away on one side, then the line of centers is disturbed causing it to bend sharply to the right or left as the case may be.

As the two sides of the belly are ground away, an important condition arises which we will call "belly angle" (Fig. 10). The amount of belly angle depends entirely on how much metal is ground away on both sides. Belly angle is a very important feature, since it directly involves "lift" (Fig. 10C).

A. FOR WIDE SHADE LINES AND SHALLOW CUTTING.
B. FOR DEEPER CUTTING; NOT SO WIDE.
C. FOR A DEEP CUT ; NARROW.

FIG. 9.

Lift decides for you how high or low you must hold your graver to the article or plate when making a cut. This should be carefully studied and experimented with, because herein lies the source of most graver troubles. You would find that a very low degree of lift or belly angle will cause difficulty in cutting. Also an extremely high degree is next to impossible to handle. The reader will find his happy medium through experimenting. In discussing lift, it is in relation to average cutting on average work. As the learner progresses and begins cutting on curved surfaces, he will find the lift will have to be changed to suit the surface. Curved surfaces usually demand an increased lift whether concave or convex. Flat surfaces can be cut with a lower

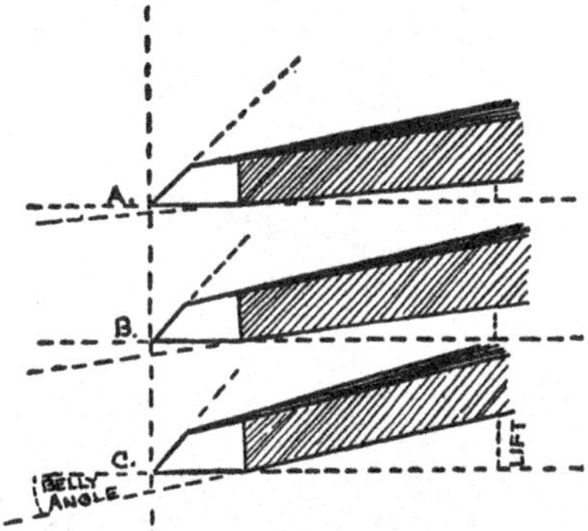

A. BELLY ANGLE SLIGHT; NOT MUCH LIFT.
B. INCREASED BELLY ANGLE ; MORE LIFT.
C. STILL MORE BELLY ANGLE RESULTING
   IN GREATLY INCREASED LIFT.

FIG. 10.

lift. The reader should adapt the graver to suit his hand. The lift for average work should be at least high enough for the engraver to get his fingers comfortably underneath the graver handle.

Fig. 11 is self-explanatory, but here a word of caution. Avoid extremes as in Fig. 11C. For average work, Fig. 11B is ideal. If Fig. 11C were matched with a belly as in Fig. 9A, the two extremes would be of no value. If a wide shade line is desired, it must be remembered that the result is obtained by altering the belly and not the face. The right edge of the graver is brought slightly forward, because all of the cutting is done on that side, and this helps the tool to cut more readily. To execute a shade line in script, the graver is laid over on the right side considerably. By bringing the right edge slightly forward (Fig. 11B) it is not necessary to lay the graver over quite so far to get the desired width of shade line.

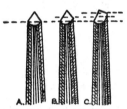

A. FOR CUTTING THIN HAIRLINES.
B. FOR SHADE CUTS OF AVERAGE WIDTH.
C. FOR WIDER SHADE LINES; BAD FOR HAIRLINES.

FIG. 11.

Fig. 12 is also self-explanatory. It is only necessary to add that a higher face angle is desired on cutting hard or tough metals. A low angle would break too many points. A graver with a low face angle cuts more readily and makes a smoother cut and should be used on all softer metals that will not endanger the point.

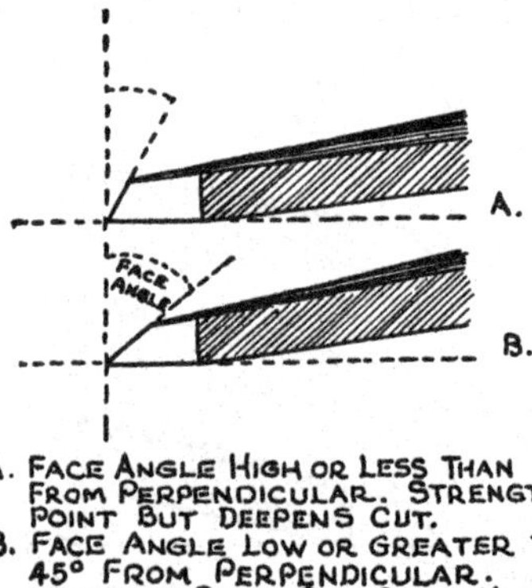

A. FACE ANGLE HIGH OR LESS THAN 45° FROM PERPENDICULAR. STRENGTHENS POINT BUT DEEPENS CUT.
B. FACE ANGLE LOW OR GREATER THAN 45° FROM PERPENDICULAR. WEAKENS POINT BUT CUTS MORE READILY AND LESS DEEP.

FIG. 12.

3. Polishing

Great care should be taken to develop correct polishing methods because therein lies the reason for the success or failure of a smoothly executed cut. Assuming that a graver has been properly faced, the problem of obtaining a good polish is undertaken. First, place the graver in the handle and polish the belly as shown in Fig. 13. This must be done by placing the side or face to be polished perfectly flat on 4-0 emery paper; pull toward you, always away from the point of the graver. Placing the fingers as shown in the

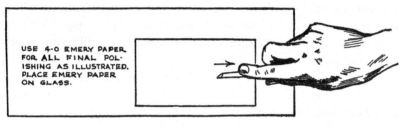

USE 4-0 EMERY PAPER
FOR ALL FINAL POL·
ISHING AS ILLUSTRATED.
PLACE EMERY PAPER
ON GLASS.

FIG. 13.

illustration, press lightly as the motion is begun. In polishing thusly, always place the emery paper over the glass piece or section over which the graver sharpener slides when facing gravers. This guarantees a firm, hard, and smooth surface which will minimize the risk of rounding the edges.

Short careful strokes of about one-half inch in length are more easily controlled than long strokes and the risk of rounding the edges is reduced. However, the beginner must be very preserving in this particular task. This is hand work and requires skill to execute successfully. Much practice is required before a beginner can complete the job without rounding the edges. Many strokes are not necessary. A few slow, careful strokes are enough to insure an adequate polish. The amount of hand polishing will depend to a degree on the fineness of the Arkansas stone.

It is advisable when polishing new faces to use a fresh piece of emery paper. The first polishing stroke will leave a trail on the paper, which should show an even stroke, perfectly uniform. If the graver face is not contacting the emery paper in a flat position, the trail will show deeper on one side than on the other. This demands an immediate correction if rounded edges are to be avoided.

After a considerable amount of practice, the student will develop in his finger tips a "feel" or "touch" for flatness and this "feel" may be relied upon more and more as experience is gained.

Among finished engravers, different viewpoints are often held on polishing methods. Many contend the correct way to polish the belly is to drag the graver sideways, away from the point, over the emery paper. In this manner the motion of the strokes is parallel to the cutting edges. This method is very good; results are excellent, but beginners usually have great difficulty in preserving flat faces. It is not suggested that beginners try this method until more experience is acquired.

How much to polish the faces? Looking down at the two sides or faces of the belly, the left side is the cutting edge and deserves more attention. This face should receive more actual polishing or rubbing on emery. The edge must be smooth, free of scratches and burrs. The right face may be polished just enough to remove lines and burrs created by the stones. The one face on top of the graver, "the face" of the tool, does not necessarily require any polishing other than that done on the Arkansas stone. If burrs are showing on this face, it is naturally wise to rub it over emery paper once or twice but not for the purpose of polishing. Remember that a brilliant cut depends on the brilliance of the polish on the left side of the belly (the left side of the belly when viewing both sides at once becomes the right side when in actual cutting position). Acquiring a high polish on the face is not only of no real value, but is generally detrimental to good results.

To summarize, the left face of the belly (viewing both sides) receives more polishing attention; the right side of the belly is less important, and "the face" of the graver receives little or no polishing on emery paper.

In following the program outline up to this point, the reader has become familiar with such essential equipment as the engraving block, gravers, oilstones, graver sharpener, and emery paper. Next to consider is the engraver's magnifying eyeglass or loupe, and the metal to be cut.

The correct loupe for an engraver should allow the eye to be 4 inches from the work and magnify 2½ times. The loupe should be one that is marked 4 in. x 2½X. It is important for the beginner to make sure he has the correct loupe before attempting to cut.

The best material on which to begin practice work is commercial sheet copper, cut to any convenient size to be held in the engraving block, say about two by three inches. The trade specification for a suitable metal is: "cold-rolled flat sheet copper, polished on one side, thickness 14 ounces per square foot, or .0189 inch." This thickness is minimum for properly standing up under the graver cuts. Thicker metal may be used, but it would cost more per square inch with no advantage in working qualities. Copper of this specification has a cutting quality that is probably nearest of all to averaging that of the metals of which most articles are made, that are engraved in the jewelry trade; gold of various karat-fineness, solid or filled; silver; platinum; certain non-precious metals used as a base for electroplating, etc. Plates of this kind of copper are stocked for sale by some of the jewelers' supply dealers. However, if you buy the metal in larger sheets as sold by metal dealers, it is well to have it cut to usable size by a sheet-metal workshop on their large power-shear so that the practice plates will be perfectly flat. It is impossible to maintain flatness in pieces cut with hand shears.

FIG. 14.

FIG. 15.

FIG. 16

Holding the graver correctly is of utmost importance. The correct position is shown in Figs. 14 and 15. Fig. 16 shows the hand in relation to the copper plate and executing a straight cut. Fig. 17 shows the copper plate clamped securely in the engraving block with the aid of four small grooved pins; also showing the hands in their correct position on the block preparatory to making a cut.

FIG. 17. One of two correct positions of hands for beginning all cutting.

Figs. 17 and 18 show correct hand posture for beginning all cutting. The difference in the thumb positions should be noted in the two illustrations. Both are correct. As cutting progresses, the student may unconsciously find himself changing from one position to the other. For extra steadiness, the left thumb serves this purpose well.

Fig. 19 shows the engraver with elbows resting on the table top, arms relaxed, with the block slightly tilted toward his body. The chair or stool should never be so high as to cause the engraver to be directly over his work; neither should it be so low that it would become necessary to overtilt the block in order to approach the work. Bad posture

FIG. 18. Alternative position has thumbs together on work for extra steadiness.

FIG. 19. Correct posture for engraving.

causes early fatigue. The engraver should keep his spine as straight as possible by selecting a chair or stool of just the right height.

Before beginning to cut, study Figs. 20 and 21. Consider first Fig. 20: (A) shows the correctly shaped cut; (B) shows a cross-section of the depth of the cut, lengthwise; and (C) shows a cross-section of the width and depth of the cut. Fig. 21 shows the cut in execution. The procedures and methods of executing this particular cut are explained later, in detail, under item 12 of the text. It is mentioned here, in brief, to establish in the beginner's mind a clear conception of what actually happens as the graver point cuts the metal.

FIG. 20. Correctly shaped cut (A). B and C show lengthwise and width cross-sections.

4. Cutting Parallel Straight Lines

Lay out a practice plate with four equal rows of diagonal straight lines as shown in Fig. 22A. This is done by smearing on

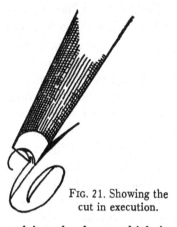

FIG. 21. Showing the cut in execution.

Chinese white, a water-color manufactured in cake form, which is applied by wetting the forefinger with water and rubbing over the cake. The finger will pick up the Chinese white as a thick paste which is rubbed on the plate, continuing to rub until dry. This will leave a thin creamy coat of white and will avoid scaling, which greatly interferes with cutting. With a ruler, lay out four equal rows parallel with the long edge of the copper plate. On the top row, lay out a series of

FIG. 22. Metal plate layout for practicing the cutting of rows of parallel lines.

close, parallel diagonal lines. This may be done with a steel point or a hard lead pencil, finely pointed. Care must be taken not to bear down on the steel point, because a deep cut or line will result. All that is necessary is to lightly touch the surface. A faint but definite line will result, which is ideal. If the steel point is used, the Chinese white may then be removed and the lines cut. If the lead pencil is used the cutting is done directly over the Chinese white.

The first plate should be cut just to get the feel of the copper with no particular emphasis on the desired width of line. Cutting these straight lines does not involve turning the block. All the action is in sliding the graver past the thumb which remains stationary. To cut perfectly straight lines, hold the block steady with the left hand and rest the thumb of the right hand on the top of the block. The right thumb must not move. The graver slides past the thumb in a continuous smooth motion. The tip of the forefinger must be placed on the graver at least an inch from the tip of the thumb. This is necessary to execute a long straight cut in one stroke. If the graver is in perfect condition, it will glide through the metal smoothly and with little resistance.

An important rule at this point is to "wait for the metal to cut." Do not force the graver to cut faster than it should. A graver in perfect condition will start cutting as soon as the point touches the metal and a minimum of pressure is used. This may be fast or slow depending on the graver. In either event the result will be a smooth cut, if the graver is not hurried or forced. The next step is to lay out a plate of the same parallel lines but this time try to cut a thin even line from start to finish. When this can be done some control has been acquired.

5. Cutting Curved Parallel Lines

Lay out a plate with four rows. See Fig. 22B. Using a coin and the steel point or pencil as a marker, lay out a series of close parallel arcs. To cut an arc, the block must be turned slightly as the thumb pivots. The graver is held firmly and there is no action of the graver sliding past the thumb. At this point it is well to form the habit of shifting the copper plate from time to time so that all cutting is done as close to the axis of the block as possible. This simplifies cutting near the edges of the plate. If the plate is not moved toward center, the arc or motion of the block is amplified causing unnecessary difficulties in cutting.

6. Cutting Circles in Hair-lines

With a compass, lay out two sets of circles on one side of a plate. This is shown in Fig. 23. Each set should contain a series of circles gradually diminishing in size to center. Many more lines may be worked in than are shown in the illustration. It is advisable to place the lines as close as possible in order that a maximum amount of cutting may be gotten from one plate. In cutting these, try to maintain a very light hairline (Fig. 23A). This will involve changing position in turning the block, to complete the circle. Do this in no more than four turns.

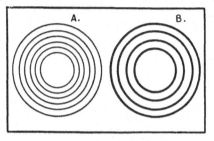

Fig. 23. Practice plate for cutting hairline and shaded circles.

7. Cutting Parallel Shaded Lines

Lay out a plate as shown in Fig. 22C. This time, in cutting a line, lay the graver over to the right and cut a straight shade line of even width from beginning to end. It will be found that in order to do this the point of the graver must go a little deeper into the copper plate. A maximum shade width is wanted here. By maximum width is meant the widest possible line that can be controlled. After a few practice cuts, starting fairly narrow and gradually widening as experience is gained, it will seem comparatively easy to maintain the even width desired until a great width is reached. Then it will be found the outer edges of the shade lines become uneven, feathery, or ragged. This is quite a natural condition and is merely an indication that too wide a shade line has been attempted.

8. Cutting Curved Parallel Shaded Lines

Lay out a plate as shown in Fig. 22D. On this plate, cut shaded arcs of maximum width.

9. Cutting Shaded Circles

Lay out a plate as shown in Fig. 23B. Cut shaded circles of maximum width.

10. Cutting Script Ovals—Hairlines

Lay out a plate of four rows. See Fig. 24A. Before designing the script ovals shown in the illustration, it is necessary to establish the correct script slant. At the beginning of each row construct a perfect square. Divide into four equal sections and connect the lower

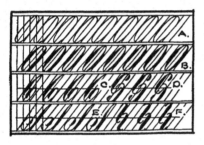

FIG. 24. Practice plate for cutting script letters.

left corner point with the top third line point. This is correct script slant. Then draw a series of lines on each row parallel to the first or script slant line. These lines are used to guide your cutting and keep all slanted shade lines parallel. Design a series of ovals, freehand, taking care to make them perfectly symmetrical and slender. This design is done with a finely pointed pencil. After completing the design of a complete row of ovals, it is safer to make the design permanent by tracing lightly with the steel point. Cut them with light hair-lines, being particularly careful in making the short turns at the top and bottom. The beginner must learn to make these turns without burring the edges of the cut.

11. Cutting Script Ovals—Shaded

Lay out another plate of four rows. Design script ovals in the same manner as described for item 10. See Fig. 24B. These lines must start at the top as a hair-line; gradually increase the width until a full shade is reached about half-way down. At this point gradually diminish or taper out the lines. When the point of the graver is lifted out of the metal, a hair-line should have been reached again. The principle of the cut is to taper from a hair-line into a full shade and out again into a hair-line. In actual cutting, the graver is rolled over to the right and rolled back straight or upright at the end of the cut. The return cut from the bottom is executed in the same manner. The up-cut is started where the down-cut ended and ends where the down-cut began. A skilled engraver will show no gaps between cuts. Care must be taken that the top and bottom of the oval does not become pointed. To keep them properly rounded, the individual cut must begin with a decided but short hair-line curve. This shade cut is by far the most important and difficult cut to be mastered, and deserves much attention and practice. The greatest number of cuts in the script alphabet are identical with this cut, and vary only in size.

12. Shading Beauty-cut

The beauty-cut is shown in Fig. 24C for plate lay-out and in Fig. 25 for direction of cutting. The beauty-cut forms the principal part of many script capitals. It is cut much in the same manner as the shaded script oval previously explained. Three separate cuts are necessary. Starting at the top of the line a long shade cut is executed, reaching its greatest width

FIG. 25.

very slightly below the center line and tapering out of the cut until the tool is lifted just before reaching the lower line. Start here with a light hair-line and cut upward to the center line. The last short shade line is started at the end of the previous hair-line cut. The cut is comparatively straight on the inside or graver point side, and nicely rounded on the outside or shallow edge of the cut.

The order of cutting may be changed to slight advantage if the reader wishes. The two shade lines may be cut first and the hair-line connection last. The advantage in this method is in keeping the shade lines parallel.

Another acceptable way to do this figure is by using only two cuts altogether. The first cut is the long shade line downward; the second cut begins with the hair-line cutting upward and continuing into the final shorter shade cut without lifting the graver until the end of the shade line. The latter method requires a greater degree of skill since more motion is involved in turning the block and the last shade line must fall exactly parallel to the first. The result, however, is gratifying when successfully accomplished.

13. Shading Beauty-stem

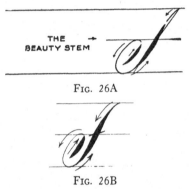

FIG. 26A

FIG. 26B

The beauty-stem is shown in Fig. 24 E for plate lay-out and in Fig. 26 A for direction of cutting. This cut varies slightly from the script oval cut or beauty-cut. The first cut is the short center shade-cut. The second is a hair-line that picks up at the tip of the first cut, swings completely around and broadens into a full shade cut as it becomes parallel with the script slant. At the top, the figure bends slightly to the right so it is necessary to lift up the graver before reaching the top of the figure. The third cut starts at the top of the line, comes down to meet and blend into the up-cut. The reason for three cuts on this figure is because on the up-cut the figure bends in a clockwise direction and all engraving is done counter-clockwise.

See Fig. 26B for an alternate method of cutting the beauty-stem. Many engravers like the two cuts in the main stem to meet nearer the center rather than blend the hairline into the stem at the top. The cut is more intricate since the two shade cuts must be precisely the same width as they meet. The effect is beautiful, much like the double-cut. The beginner may wish to attempt this cut after mastering the simpler method shown in Fig. 26A.

14. Shading Double-C Cuts

The linked design or double "C" cut is shown in Fig. 24D for plate lay-out and in Fig. 27 for direction of cutting, and contains one troublesome cut for the beginner. This is the first short shade cut or tip, formed at the beginning of each link or "C" cut. The difficulty is in obtaining a maximum shade width in so short a cut. The graver must be laid over and immediately lifted out, in one continuous motion. The other composite cuts offer no new treatment. Direction of cutting is shown in Fig. 27.

15. Shading Double-cut

The double-cut is made in four cuts. See Fig. 24F for plate lay-out and Fig. 28 for directions of cutting. Starting just below center of the figure, a short wide shade is made upward, then a short shade line of the same width is made downward. The tips are finished off

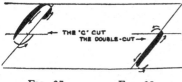

FIG. 27.   FIG. 28.

FIG. 29. Side and top views of common errors in executing cuts.

with a curved hair-line. The great difficulty in executing this cut is in fitting the two shade lines together.

In completing this chapter the reader's attention is directed mainly to securing a well-formed shade line and a thin hair-line. Of the two, the well-formed shade line is most difficult. The common errors shown in Fig. 29 will be of value in locating imperfections of a consistent nature. Fig. 29A shows an incorrectly executed cut with too much depth at the end of the cut. See A1 for top view. Fig. 29B shows an incorrect cut with too much depth and width at the beginning of the cut. See B1 for top view. Fig. 29C shows an incorrect cut with a wavy line and uneven depth. See C1 for top view. To see how the double-cut is used in capital letters refer to Fig. 32, letters "R - U - Y and K." Then, refer to Fig. 33 to see how the double-cut is used in lower-case letters "h - k - m - n - p and v."

Chapter 2

Cutting Script Letters

1. Drawing (on paper) script alphabet and numerals; study of proportion of letters to each other.
2. Cutting script capital letters.
3. Cutting script lower case.
4. Cutting script numerals.
5. Cutting script names, dates, inscriptions.
6. Cutting script two letter monograms.
7. Cutting script three-letter monograms.
8. Cutting drop-script two-letter monograms.
9. Cutting drop-script three-letter monograms.
10. Cutting diagonal drop-script monograms.

IN FOLLOWING this plan for learning to do artistic engraving, it is well now and then to take a little time off from the work of the moment to consider how the latter is related to the work of other sections of the course; those that have been accomplished and the one next in line to be begun. This occasional orientation promotes a more thorough grasp of the principles underlying the work of the course and a quicker accomplishment of practical ability.

In Chapter 1, items 1 to 15 inclusive, you have presumably mastered the shaping and sharpening of the square script graver, and the use of it in cutting only the simple elements of which all script letters are composed. Our experience has indicated that it is best to place this elementary tool work ahead of the subject of drawing for sound pedagogical reasons, even though, obviously, the drawing of the "copy" has to be done on articles to be engraved, before they can be cut with tools. So now your instruction in *drawing* the plain script alphabet, capitals and lower case, and numerals, with pencil on paper, is the next thing to begin. This is labeled as step 1 on our list. Steps 2 through 10 provide next for thorough development of ability in *cutting* this basic script alphabet on copper plates. The "feel" in using the square script graver is very nearly the same in engraving on copper as on gold, silver, or metals of the platinum group.

The standard script alphabet is the foundation on which ability in all other forms of engraving must be built. As "the carpenter is known by his chips," so the engraver is known by his script. The elements of script letters are simple and stand out nakedly to be judged; not like in the massed lines in fancy monograms and decorative work, among which some more or less faulty cutting can be easily camouflaged, but only to the uncritical eye. We urge the reader to devote much time and effort to practicing drawing the script alphabet units with pencil on paper. Do not be in a great hurry to combine the drawing with cutting it on copper; that is naturally a temptation to the beginner but one will go farther toward proficiency in any given length of time by restraining his urge to *cut* script until he can *draw* it well.

In your first attempts, you can hardly avoid excessive cautiousness in the use of the pencil, making your copy with short strokes, "pecking" at it, in a sort of timidity or fear that you might overrun the required pencil line. But one should recognize that this is a drawback and try to acquire reasonably soon the knack of making longer strokes with more freedom and certainty of movement of the pencil. Let your practice include the gradual cultivation of a confident boldness with the pencil. In time this should lead to both a good style and a greater speed and output of work. The same principle underlies practicing for efficient cutting with the graver.

Before beginning to design on paper, consider first the type of paper and pencil to be used. Any firm white paper with not too smooth a surface will serve well. An exceptionally rough surface, while good for suggesting form, is a poor medium for adding fine detail and should be avoided.

For large practice designing on paper, a grade No. 2 lead pencil may be used to sketch in the form of the letters. A No. 4 lead pencil, which is somewhat harder, may then be used for the more accurate shaping and adding of details. These are rather soft pencils and hence should be used only for designing on paper. Some engravers prefer to use a pencil for designing directly on the work to be engraved rather than to use a hard rubber point or "stylus." In this case, a very hard pencil, at least a 6 H, should be used, because anything softer will not hold the fine point that is so necessary. In using a pencil to design directly on the work, it must be understood that there is some risk of scratching the surface to be cut, since the fine point of a hard lead pencil acts much in the same manner as the steel point of a stylus.

1. Drawing Script Alphabet and Numerals

Design on paper the "Simplified Script Alphabet" (Fig. 30) and numerals using the script slant lines to keep all shade lines parallel. A convenient way to lay out the script slant line is to shape one end of a plastic or celluloid ruler with the desired slant of 54 degrees. Using this gauge, the lines may be quickly and easily placed without constructing the usual square at the beginning of each row of letters. This first alphabet is the simplest form of script. The basic proportions of each letter should be closely studied. Fig. 31 shows the fundamental construction "key" for each letter and numeral. The key deals only with the body form. Careful study of Fig. 31 will show that even the most complicated letters in appearance can be broken down into simple basic forms. Once this is understood, designing technique will develop rapidly. Carefully note the comparative sizes of the capitals, lower case, and numbers. The lower case letters are 1/3 to 1/2 the height of the capital letters. The numbers are 2/3 the height of the capital letters.

When this alphabet is mastered in design, the more complicated "Leonard Script Alphabet" will come easily (Fig. 34A and Fig. 34B). The construction is the same with the addition of hair-lines used for artistic effect and beauty.

It must be realized that before any cutting is attempted the student must fully understand the nature of the design. Cutting a poor design is time wasted with nothing gained. Good cutting depends on good design and contrary to popular belief among beginners, the mechanics of simple cutting can be learned and executed with some degree of skill in a comparatively short time. The beginner usually feels that he must concentrate on the cutting and that

FIG. 30. Simplified script.

alone, with the idea that the designing will come in time. It is far
better to reverse the idea; concentrate on the designing and the cutting will come in time. Too much emphasis cannot be placed on designing and the student should approach each new phase with this
in mind.

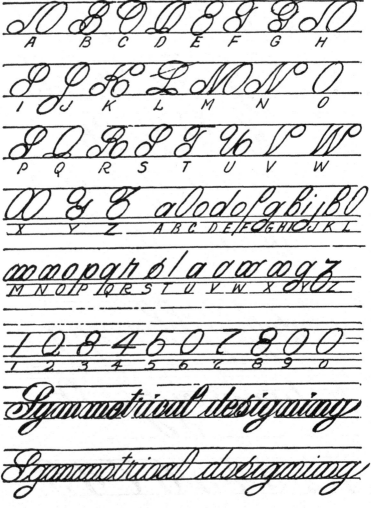

Fig. 31. Designing key for each letter.

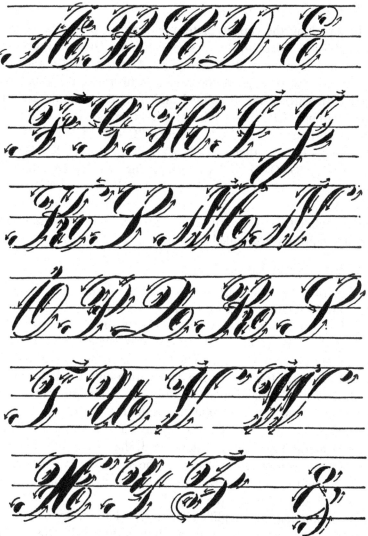

Fig. 32. Script capitals, showing direction of cutting.

2. Cutting Script Capitals

In designing the copper plate, preparatory to cutting, it is well to establish a maximum letter size. Cutting a letter in excess of ⅜ inches in height demands a shade line of extreme width and should not be attempted. A good standard size to use is a ⁵⁄₁₆-inch letter height. In cutting the simplified alphabet, the capitals are taken first in groups that have similar construction. See Fig. 32 for direction of cutting. First, take the letters, "C - F - L - S - T"; next, "D - I - J - P - Y"; then "M - N - V - W"; "B - H - K - R"; "A - X - E - G"; "O - Q - U - Z." On completing the capital letters, the next step is to cut a plate of Leonard script capital letters (Fig. 34A). Remember, there is no variation in original construction of the two alphabets. Leonard script appears more elaborate simply because hairlines are added.

3. Cutting Script Lower Case

In cutting the lower-case letters there are certain similar groups. They are as follows: a - c - e - o, m - n - v - w, b - d - f - h -k - l - t, g - j - p - q - y - z, r - s - u - x - i. The "a - n - m - v - w - d - h - k - t - g - j - p - q - y - u and i" contain raw shade cuts that should be squared off with a "pick." The "pick" is made exactly the same in each letter, so to simplify the explanation only the letter "i" will be discussed. To make a lower case "i," a straight cut is made downward. It will be seen that the beginning of the cut looks raw and unfinished. It is necessary to "square off" the cut with a "pick." Starting at the top right, cut downward, diagonally into the shade cut. Lift out as soon as the center of the shade cut is reached. This "pick" should form a little triangle with sides nearly equal. See Fig. 33 immediately following the letter "z."

On completing the simplified lower case letters, lay out and cut a plate of Leonard script lower case letters. Fig. 34B. Observe such minor variations as they occur at the tip of the "b - v and w." Note also the slight change in construction of the "p" and "q."

4. Cutting Script Numerals

The simplified numbers may be taken in order noting the unusual construction on the bottom of the "2," the bar on the "4," the top of the "7." See Fig. 33 for direction of cutting. The stem of the "1" and "4" is started at the bottom, cutting upward. The bottom of the "2" is made in two cuts to get a gradual curve. The top of the "7"

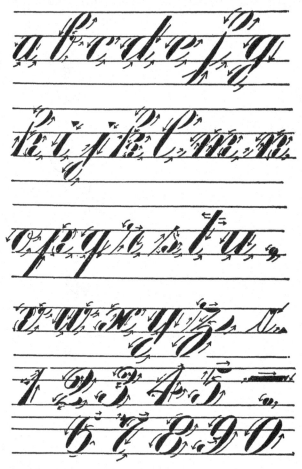

Fig. 33. Simplified lower case script letters and numerals showing direction of cutting.

is done like the bottom of the "2" with the addition of a tiny pick cutting upward. After completing the simplified numbers, lay out and cut the Leonard script numbers. The variations found here offer a more pleasing and artistic style with no extra cutting difficulty.

5. Cutting Script Names, Dates, Inscriptions

In cutting names much has to be learned about spacing. It must also be learned at this point that good cutting cannot save a poor

Fig. 34A. Leonard script capitals.

design. To become familiar with script spacing, it is best to take pencil and paper and begin by designing single names accurately, using script slant lines. Design the capital letter first and then design the lower case letters 1/3 to 1/2 the size of the capitals. Close spacing between letters is more desirable in script. Wide spacing between letters is difficult to keep regular. The letter immediately following the capital should be placed close by without cramping. The letter should not connect with the capital but should start from a hair-line as in "Thomas," shown in Fig. 34B. The remaining letters in the name should be spaced closely and regularly. All shade lines must be parallel. This is the secret of cutting good, regular script. Certain letters like the "R" and "H" seem to push the lower case letters away because of their construction. Here, again, close spacing is urged to prevent a gap between the capital and the following lower case letter. Spacing in script is not mechanical but optical, meaning that to space correctly one must depend entirely on judgment by eye. Each word presents a different spacing problem because of the different combination of letters. If the reader is searching for an ironclad rule or key to correct spacing, there is none. The solution is practice and familiarization with every conceivable letter combination. After considerable preliminary designing, try cutting a few names. Begin with a maximum size, gradually diminishing. The beginner is hardly expected to do exceptionally small work so early in the course. Lower case letters as small as 1/32 inch are often used in practical work and it is suggested that the inexperienced engraver attempt to cut as near to this size as he possibly can.

When designing it is best to use a single line. In the cutting, the final result will be closer spacing than expected and considerable practice and experience is necessary to "get the knack of it."

After this, full names should be designed and cut. In centering a full name and date on a plate, find by measurement the actual center of the plate and draw a line (see Fig. 34B). Count the letters in the name "Jerry R. Cox" and count the two spaces as letters. This makes eleven spaces and the sixth space is the approximate center. Starting with the "R," design to the right. Starting with the "y" in "Jerry," design backward to the left. Use the same procedure on "April 23, 1946." With a little practice, this method will prove fast and accurate. Allowances will naturally be made for narrow letters such as "I" or "T," or the number "1." This can be taken into consideration before sketching the design.

In designing a five-line inscription on a plate, see Fig. 35A, the same procedure is used on spacing and centering the letter on the individual lines, but first the lines have to be centered. To do this,

Fig. 34B. Leonard Script lower case letters, numerals and names.

find the horizontal center as well as the vertical center. The third line will naturally fall on center and that line is placed first. Then the second and fourth lines are equally placed above and below. Then, the first and fifth lines are placed respectively. The wording on each line is sketched in, the design steel pointed and cut. Figs. 35B and 35C show the lay-out for four-line and three-line inscriptions.

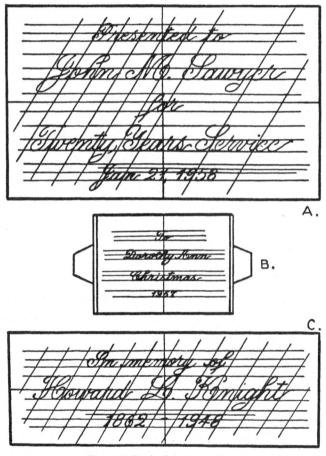

Fig. 35. Designing inscriptions.

6. Cutting Two-letter Monograms

To design script two-letter monograms, study Fig. 36. This suggests how two or three running script letters may be connected simply. Here different combinations present different problems so there is really no exact rule. Practice in design is the only answer. Balance of design is essential in this type of monogram and the effect should be like the "CB" at the bottom of Fig. 36. Some script letters will loop themselves quite naturally; some will not loop at all; some require considerable time and redesigning to get a balanced design. On those that will not loop, the best that can be done is to arrange them symmetrically close together and the result will be satisfactory.

On a problem combination, the best method is to roughly design it on paper. Note how the letters fall naturally. Then without erasing this design, lay out another beside it. Try to improve this one. Then, leaving this design, try another, gradually improving each one until a satisfactory design results. This may take four to ten separate sketches, but it is the only way to handle a problem monogram. The advantage in this method is in keeping all of your ideas and attempts in front of you. Trying to touch up an original design by erasing usually ends up in a poor design.

In cutting connected letters, the following rules must be observed. A shade line must not cross a shade line. A shade line may cross a hair-line. The lines crossing must appear to go over and under. A hair-line must never be cut directly across a shade line.

In cutting these designs, follow the procedure of beginning with a maximum letter size, decreasing gradually to smaller sizes.

7. Cutting Three-letter Monograms

The technique in designing three-letter monograms is the same as explained under topic 6 of the step procedure. It involves one other principle—equally spacing the individual letter stems. This must be done by eye and must be observed closely or unequal spacing will result. The alphabet as connected in three letter groups (Fig. 36) is a fair example of even spacing.

In cutting three-letter monograms, begin with large letters (approximately 5/16 inches in height) and reduce gradually.

8. Cutting Drop-script Two-letter Monograms

Referring to Fig. 36, two-letter drop monograms can be laid out and connected as shown on the extreme left. Different combinations will present individual problems and they can all be worked out in the same manner as explained under item 6 in the list. The principle of laying out a two-letter drop monogram involves working from a center vertical line. The stems of the individual letters must be in line. It is not necessary for the outer parts of the letters to line up.

9. Cutting Drop-script Three-letter Monograms

Designing three-letter drop-script monograms becomes more complicated in construction. Begin the lay-out by finding the center by using a vertical and a horizontal line. Decide on the desired height of the center letter. From this, the construction lines for the top and bottom letters may be accurately placed. Estimate first how far down into the center letter the top letter will merge. Place a horizontal line at this point, also. It follows, of course, that the top and bottom letters are exactly the same height of the center letter and may be measured, thus locating the two remaining construction lines.

10. Cutting Diagonal Drop-script Monograms

Diagonal drop-script monograms include two types of designs, one developing to the left, the other developing to the right. This is shown at the bottom of Fig. 36 in the two designs of the combination "L. R. H." The design developing to the right is most used and has no constructional similarity to the design developing to the left. The design to the right follows a stepped-down procedure as shown in the illustration; it is constructed similarly to the vertical drop monograms completed in item 9 of the list heading Chap. 2.

The design to the left is easily understood and executed if one simple rule is observed. The letters must never slant to the left of the vertical center construction line. They should instead be vertical or slant very slightly to the right.

Design and cut several letter combinations of both right and left developments. Begin with a maximum letter size and gradually decrease the over-all size of the monograms.

In concluding the instruction on script, it may be mentioned that the two alphabets discussed (simplified script and Leonard script) are not presumed to be the only acceptable script alphabets. To the

FIG. 36. Script combinations.

contrary, there are many other highly acceptable alphabets with very pleasing variations. Simplified script and Leonard script are chosen as examples because of their relative and simple basic construction from which the reader may vary his own personal style.

A recommended variation of a simple script alphabet is shown in Fig. 37. The style is light and airy, and in actual cutting is most pleasing to the eye.

FIG. 37. A variation of simple script.

Chapter 3

Cutting Ribbon Letters

THE RIBBON ALPHABET is so-called because its design and method of cutting is intended to resemble real folds of ribbon. It has been in use for generations, trending from the plainer treatments to even more complex and ornate renditions. Fig. 38 is presented as a basic, authentic treatment of this elaborate alphabet. The ribbon alphabet as it is presented here is invaluable to the beginner in learning engraving for several reasons. Much cutting practice is gained; technique in design is developed to a high degree; a background is formed from which the engraver may vary the style or design to suit his own purposes.

The ribbon alphabet introduces a system of cutting that may be adapted to many other simpler alphabets, on which instruction will be given in later pages of this book; hence the placement of the ribbon style next in importance to slanted script. It will also be

36

interesting to note how important a part it will play later on as a foundation for the work of Chapters 8 and 9.

1. Ribbon Letter Alphabet; Drawing Principles

Design on paper the "Ribbon Alphabet" as shown in Fig. 38. In designing a letter, a good plan to follow is the point system, always working from center. It should be understood that in order to design

FIG. 38. Ribbon alphabet.

successfully, a critical eye must be developed and the secret lies in being able to judge comparative distances or spaces from point to point. For example, on the ribbon letter "L," Fig. 39, construct a perpendicular line that splits the center stem. Construct three horizontal lines representing the top, bottom and center of the letter. Design the stem, noting that the swing to the top left is equal to the

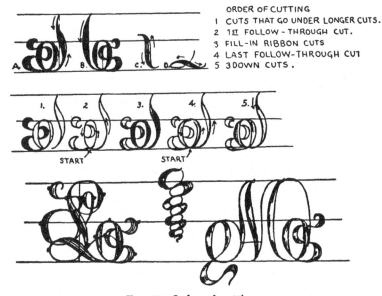

ORDER OF CUTTING
1 CUTS THAT GO UNDER LONGER CUTS.
2 1ST FOLLOW - THROUGH CUT.
3 FILL-IN RIBBON CUTS
4 LAST FOLLOW-THROUGH CUT
5 3 DOWN CUTS.

Fig. 39. Order of cutting.

swing to the bottom right. The distances to the right and left may be located by eye, placing a dot or point with a pencil. The complete stem may be drawn from top to bottom. It will be noted that the top of the "L" develops into an oval and it is determined how far over to the right the oval swings by placing a point at its outer edge. Draw in the oval. The bottom of the "L" has an individual construction and can be compared to a horizontal figure eight. The outer distances are located equi-distant from the vertical stem. Place two points at the outermost edges of the figure eight. Design a symmetrical figure eight. Now the letter proper is complete. It only remains to locate the smaller curves. The right loop of the figure eight is extended upward to a point located just above the horizontal center line. The locations of the smaller loops are located by points, estimating their respective positions in relation to the center horizontal line and the bottom horizontal line. Of the three smaller loops, located at the lower right of the "L," the one in the middle is closer to the center line, and its respective position is so located. The smallest loop is clearly seen to swing just above the center horizontal line so its point location is easily determined. It remains to connect these points with a single line and last sketch in the width or shaded portions. Now, the loop in the upper left of the "L" develops from the oval already constructed at the upper right. The outer edges of these loops are located in the same manner as the loops at the lower right. The letter is now complete, and it only remains to check all oval forms to make sure there are no flat spots. Carefully round up the whole design.

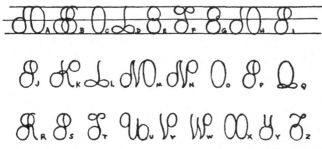

FIG. 40. In designing, letters are broken down into their simplest forms.

In designing the other letters, always break them down into their simplest forms as in Fig. 40. The letters "B-E-G and S" can be constructed using the figure eight. The "C-O and Q" are simple symmetrical ovals. The "M-N-V-W" have identical stems. The "A-H-K and R" are basic constructions of two beauty stems combined. The "F-I-J-P-T and Y" are variations of the same beauty stem. The "D-U-Z and L" have individual formations.

The "K-E-B-R" are best constructed by locating the center oval on top of the center horizontal line. The "M" and "W" have two sets of parallel lines; the "V" and "N," one set. If the design on these four letters does not appear symmetrical, it is usually because the stem lines are not *parallel* from top to bottom.

2. Cutting Ribbon Alphabet

The cutting on ribbons appears confusing. See Fig. 39. This is because there is so much cutting to be done on one letter and the cuts are placed very precisely. In reality, the system of cutting is quite definite and easy to follow. First, practice must be done on the two beauty stems and two double cuts (A-B-C and D of Fig. 39). The stem that makes up the left side of the letter "A" will be discussed first. The design is constructed as previously described. The small loops are cut first since they appear to run underneath the larger cuts. See Order of Cutting, Fig. 39, step 1. Gaps are left for the longer cuts to run through. In cutting, a series of shade cuts are placed so closely together that each cut barely trims the outer edge of the previous cut. Five to seven cuts are permissible on large letters. A better effect is obtained with the minimum number. Now begin cutting on the stem. The first cut is a follow-through cut, beginning at the bottom (Fig. 39, step 2), complete the oval and swing up into the long stem. Go upward as far as possible. When it becomes necessary to turn in a clockwise direction, lift the graver out. Start again at the bottom and make three fill-in cuts (Fig. 39, step 3); on the other side make three fill-in cuts; on the long stem, make three fill-in cuts; the last cut is a follow-through cut starting at the bottom line and skirting the outer edge of all previous cuts (Fig. 39, step 4), swinging from the oval into the long stem and lifting up as before. Now, make three light cuts down to meet the long stem and the figure is finished (Fig. 39, step 5).

The stem on the right of the letter "A" (Fig. 39B) is cut in the same manner. The double-cut as in the lower right of the "R" (Fig. 39C) is cut in the same manner. It requires added skill to pick up and blend each individual double-cut. When finished with this figure, the double-cut should show definitely. No attempt is made to camouflage it. In the bottom of the "D" and "L" (Fig. 39D) another double-cut is used, but this cut is camouflaged. It is necessary to hide this double-cut because of the line passing underneath. When these detail figures have been practiced and are understood, it is advisable to go right into cutting the entire alphabet. Cutting and designing can be worked out at the same time. By the time the end of the alphabet is reached, the cutting should be under full control and smooth in appearance. In cutting the alphabet, use letters about three-fourths of an inch in height.

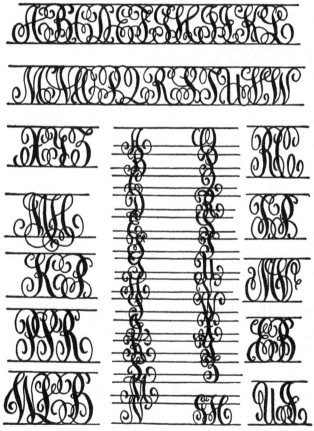

FIG. 41. Ribbon script combinations.

3. Drawing Two-letter Ribbon Monograms

Refer to Figure 41 for monogram suggestions. As in script monograms, different letter combinations present various problems and it is impossible to present all of them because the number would run well into the thousands. The best that can be offered is a series of suggested looping arrangements and the reader is advised to spend considerable time designing combinations.

Design on paper two-letter ribbon monograms connecting as shown in Figure 41.

4. Cutting Two-letter Ribbon Monograms

Cut monograms designed under item 3 only after they have been properly worked out and balanced.

5. Drawing Three-letter Ribbon Monograms

Design three-letter ribbon monograms on paper connecting as shown in Fig. 41. As in script monograms, remember the centers of each letter must be equi-distant.

6. Cutting Three-letter Ribbon Monograms

Cut monograms designed under item 5 only when the design is properly balanced and all ovals are well rounded. One important point to remember: As in script, all shades or wide lines are located parallel to each other.

7. Drawing Three-letter Drop Monograms

Design drop monograms following the same procedure as in drop script monograms. See Fig. 41 for suggested arrangements.

8. Cutting Three-letter Drop Monograms

Cut monograms designed under item 7.

9. Drawing Diagonal Drop Monograms

Design diagonal drop monograms using the same constructional techniques as explained in Chapter 2, item 10.

10. Cutting Diagonal Drop Monograms

Cut diagonal drop monograms designed under item 9.

Chapter 4

Vertical Script Letters

VERTICAL SCRIPT is a beautifully rounded and symmetrical alphabet, difficult to perfect only because the cuts are so exacting in their execution. A shaky or uncertain cut is more easily detected than in the cutting of slanted script, which fact seems to be true concerning all of the vertical single-cut alphabets.

In approaching the vertical script alphabet, think of its as primarily the same as ribbon in design, with the extra loops or "tails" eliminated. In a sense, it is stripped bare of all unnecessary ornamental additions, leaving only the essential letter formations. Since this style is always done on a much smaller scale than the ribbon alphabet, the plainness of the design enhances the beauty of the letters; any added decorative curls or loops would tend to detract from the simplicity and charm of the work.

Vertical script, while not as much in demand as slanted script, definitely has its place and must not be slighted or considered an unimportant alphabet. Instances often arise where script is wanted but the slanted style will not conform to the available space; such as on some silver flatware patterns having narrow spaces for engraving.

1. Principles of Construction

Vertical script has the same fundamental design as ribbon. See Fig. 42. The nature of cutting is the same. Only one line is used as compared with five to seven in ribbon. It is different from slanted script in cutting. All cutting in vertical script is continuous until a

Fig. 42. Vertical script.

clockwise turn is encountered, then the graver is lifted. In slanted script the graver is lifted at the end of each shade line. Vertical script is easier to cut and presents a better appearance if designed much rounder than slanted script. The short turns are more easily made on a circle than on a slender oval. In cutting, the main thing to learn is how to start from a hair-line, roll the graver over into a wide shade line, and roll back to a hair-line and again into a shade line and so on.

Three-sixteenths of an inch is the maximum height for vertical script alphabet; if in practice larger letters are required, a ribbon cut would be more advisable.

2. Cutting Capital Letters

Before cutting capital letters in the vertical script alphabet practice the usual constructional stems and double cuts shown in Fig. 39 A, B, C, and D. When these are mastered, make a plate of capital letters.

3. Cutting Lower Case Letters

The lower case alphabet goes well if letters are designed short and fat. Practice "a-c-e-o," "m-n-v-w," "b-d-f-h-k-l-t," "g-j-p-q-y-z," and "r-s-u-x-i." Then add the lower case to the plate on which capitals were cut.

The lower case letters may be one-third to one-half the height of the capital letters.

4. Cutting Numerals

Design and cut numerals. Add to the same plate.

The numerals are two-thirds the height of the capital letters.

5. Cutting Names and Dates

Design and cut single names, complete names, and names and dates together. Begin cutting names of maximum height, gradually reducing size until the smallest possible letters can be handled satisfactorily. Constructional layout for this type of work is exactly the same as explained and illustrated in Chapter 2, item 5.

6. Cutting Three-Letter Monograms

Design and cut three-letter monograms—large at first, gradually reducing size. Constructional layout is shown in Fig. 41.

7. Cutting Two-Letter Drop Monograms

Design and cut two-letter drop monograms. Constructional layout is shown in Fig. 41.

8. Cutting Three-Letter Drop Monograms

Design and cut three-letter drop monograms. This type of monogram is widely used and is especially adaptable to vertical script. It deserves more time and effort than any other phase of vertical script. Refer to Fig. 41 for suggested looping arrangements.

Chapter 5

Roman Letters

AT THIS STAGE in the book, the reader has covered the alphabets most difficult to learn; difficult both in design and in cutting. The script, ribbon, and vertical script alphabets involve more artistic designing than mere mechanical copying.

As an introduction into the block varieties of engraving, the Roman alphabet serves very well. It is cut to best advantage using the same script or square graver which is already familiar.

It is pointed out here that for engraving, lower-case block alphabets are rarely used; explanation will be confined to the capital letters. Under the block category will fall the Roman alphabet, Simple Block, Capped Block, and Gothic, each a distinct style.

Upon completing the Roman alphabet, experience with the square graver should be well-rounded and description of technique with differently designed block gravers will follow as an entirely new phase of the art of engraving.

1. Drawing on Paper

Design on paper the modern "Roman" alphabet and numerals. See Fig. 43. This alphabet is a standard alphabet used by printers, sign painters, card writers, etc. Refer to the designing "key" shown by the sketches in Fig. 44 for basic letter formations. The original alphabet has different proportionate widths for various letters. Artists and sign painters generally use the alphabet in its correct proportions, but this is not necessary or advisable for engravers. All letters should be made the same width except the "M" and "W." These can be slightly wider because of the four lines used. The "O" is a "danger" letter, and care should be taken that it does not appear shorter than other letters. This often occurs due to the fact that the letter touches the top and bottom line at a single point. As previously

ABCDEFGHIJ
KLMNOPQRS
TUVWXYZ, &.
1234567890

FIG. 43. Roman capitals and numerals.

stated, the lower case "Roman" alphabet is not generally used by engravers. Numerals are designed the same size as the capitals and are of uniform widths.

For general work, the letters should be designed tall; the width being about one-half of the height. Short, fat letters demand more space and space is usually limited. It should be understood that fat letters are acceptable and are often used on initials for the backs of watches or on bracelets. The student must learn to adapt the size of the letters to the given space. In discussing the Roman and other block alphabets, the vertical sections of square letters are referred to as "stems," the horizontal sections as "bars." The letter "E" would have one stem and three bars; the letter "N" would be composed of two narrow stems and one wide diagonal stem.

2. Cutting Stems and Serifs

To cut the thick stem as used for the letter "I," lay out on a practice plate two lines about one-fourth of an inch apart. Erect several perpendicular lines across the plate. Mark off the width of the letter "I" and begin cutting. See Fig. 44, steps 1, 2, 3, and 4.

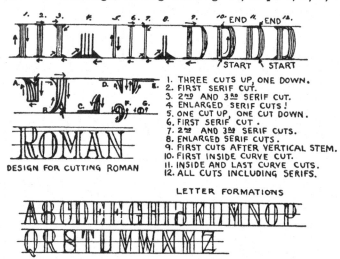

1. THREE CUTS UP, ONE DOWN.
2. FIRST SERIF CUT.
3. 2ND AND 3RD SERIF CUT.
4. ENLARGED SERIF CUTS!
5. ONE CUT UP, ONE CUT DOWN.
6. FIRST SERIF CUT.
7. 2ND AND 3RD SERIF CUTS.
8. ENLARGED SERIF CUTS.
9. FIRST CUTS AFTER VERTICAL STEM.
10. FIRST INSIDE CURVE CUT.
11. INSIDE AND LAST CURVE CUTS.
12. ALL CUTS INCLUDING SERIFS.

DESIGN FOR CUTTING ROMAN

LETTER FORMATIONS

Fig. 44. Designing key and cutting procedure for Roman alphabet.

Three shade cuts are made from the bottom up, placed closely like ribbon cuts. Then, one shade cut is made from the top down, placed closely so that no gap appears between cuts. Next, the serifs are put on to square off the ragged ends. To make a serif three cuts are used. One straight cut across the bottom of the figure to smooth out the ragged ends and give a perfectly straight base. Then, from the right make a short pick, triangular in shape, shading into the stem. From the left, make a triangular pick shading into the stem. Turn the block and cut the top serif in the same manner as the lower serif. To cut the thin or narrow stem as found in the two parallel lines in the letter "N," use one cut up and one cut down. Square off with serifs. See Fig. 44, steps 5, 6, 7, and 8.

3. Cutting Alphabet

Cut all straight letters in the alphabet first, or those without curves using a height of 5/32 of an inch. The tops of the "E-T-F-L" may prove puzzling. Refer to Fig. 44. The tip of the top bar of the letter "E" (Fig. 44D) is cut by using two cuts up into the bar and one cut down to square the edge. The bottom tip (Fig. 44C) should be a trifle larger and all three cuts are made down into the bar. The serifs are made as usual. The "F" and "L" have the same treatment.

The left tip of the top bar of the "T" (Fig. 44E) is made with three cuts upward into the bar. The right tip is made with two cuts upward and one downward to square the edge (Fig. 44D). One rule to remember is to lean shade cuts in the direction of the center of the letter. This preserves a sharp edge throughout the letter.

The curved letters which are more difficult can be cut now. A definite principle is followed here. As in the letter "D" (Fig. 44) the straight stem is cut first. Next, one cut should be made from right to left on the bottom bar (Fig. 44, step 9). Turn the block and make the same cut for the top bar. The next cut starts at the bottom of thick stem just above the first cut on the lower bar. This cut forms the side curve of the "D" and ends underneath the top bar at the thick stem (Fig. 44, step 10). Two ribbon fill-in cuts are added and the fourth cut starts at the beginning of the lower bar cut, ending at the raw edge of the top bar cut (Fig. 44, step 11). This last cut should be made very carefully as it must blend smoothly with the two bar cuts. The "B," "R," and "P" fall into this group. The "O" and "Q" are regular ribbon cuts and present nothing new.

The "C," "G," and "S" have peculiar tip treatments and should be studied separately (Fig. 44A and B). The top tip of the "C" and "G" have three cuts up and one cut down. Then one straight cut is used to square off the bottom of the four lines. Last, a tiny triangular pick is used to close up the gap at the beginning of the fourth cut down. The bottom of the "G" has three up cuts with one down cut. A half serif is used on the top of the four cuts. Close up the gap at the bottom of the down cut with the little triangular pick. The tips of the "S" are treated the same way as the tips of the "C" and "G." Note the top tip is smaller than the lower tip and the lower tip is squared off parallel with the thick stem of the letter.

The only way to design a symmetrical letter "S" is to construct first a perfect figure eight. The contours of the "S" conform perfectly with this figure. After considerable practice and study, cut the entire Roman alphabet.

FIG. 45. Slanted Roman style.

4. Cutting Numerals

After cutting the alphabet the numbers present no further problem in cutting. Care must be taken to get balance in design. Be sure numbers are of equal widths. After becoming completely familiar with the numbers, add them to the Roman alphabet plate.

5. Cutting Names, Dates, and Inscriptions

Single names should be cut first, then full names, then two line inscriptions including name and date. The spacing of Roman letters is more mechanical than script. There are certain letter groups that must be carefully watched because of their open construction on one or two sides. The "A-T-V-W-Y" are letters that are open on two sides and should be placed closer to the preceding and following letters to avoid any unsightly gaps from showing up. The "F-J-L and P" are open on one side and the preceding or following letter, as the case may be, should be moved in closer to close the natural gap and balance with the rest of the spacing. Here as in script, it must be remembered that good spacing is done by eye and not measurement; it is optical, not mechanical. One caution: parallel stems that may fall next to each other should be given a little more space to offset the optical illusion created by parallel lines. Parallel lines always appear to be closer than they really are.

In concluding instruction for the Roman alphabet, refer to Fig. 45. Shown here is a slanted style widely used and with much to be said in its favor. Designing and cutting it involves no new technique and it offers a pleasing variation of the vertical style. The vertical style is chosen for basic instruction because of its exactness; a slight error is easily detected. The slanted style does not show up an error so readily. For instance, upright lines that are slightly off parallel may not be noticed at all, due to the slant.

Chapter 6

Hardening and Tempering Steel

---

1. Principles of heat treatment as applied to making gravers and to correcting defective gravers.
2. Making a square graver: (a) filing and shaping; (b) hardening and tempering.
3. Correcting defective gravers.
4. Altering gravers for improved cutting.

AFTER READING this much of the book, the beginner has learned the primary alphabets which were cut with the script graver only. The next phase of work involves a new type of graver besides new cutting principles and demands a knowledge of heat treatment.

For engravers, the mastery of correct hardening and tempering may seem unnecessary since gravers can be bought that are supposedly just right for use. If such were the case, the engraver would not need to bother with learning the process of rehardening and tempering his gravers. But unfortunately such is not the case, and the engraver is required from time to time to temper gravers that are too hard, and sometimes to reharden gravers that are too soft.

In order to gain experience in heat-treatment the beginner may well acquire it by making script gravers from raw square steel stock. After doing this, the alterations to gravers, required in the section following this one, can be done with knowledge and skill, thereby eliminating any spoilage.

1. Principles of Heat-treatment

Correct hardening and tempering is an exacting procedure and must be carefully and accurately done. However, it is not com-

1. Select a piece of ⅛ in. square steel stock. Saw off 3¾ in. length.

2. File or grind to the above shape.

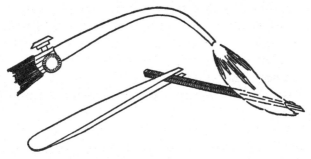

3. After applying a thin film of dampened soap over area to be hardened, heat ⅓ of length until metal is a cherry red color.

4. Plunge vertically into water or oil, taking care not to touch the sides or bottom of the container.

5. Remove scale formed by hardening with an emery stick. Heat graver over alcohol flame until the metal shows a pale straw color.

FIG. 46. How to make a graver.

plicated. Anyone, with practice, can become quite adept at it.*

"The property of tool steel to which it owes its great value is its capability of being hardened to such a degree as to enable it to cut and shape almost every known substance, including itself in its unhardened condition. This hardening is brought about by bringing a piece of steel to a red heat and plunging it into cold water or otherwise suddenly cooling it. The higher the proportion of carbon in the steel, the harder will this heating and quenching leave it. After hardening, the metal is found to be too brittle for most purposes, so it has to be subjected to a tempering process or 'letting down' to the proper degree of hardness, according to the purpose intended. This tempering consists simply in slowly reheating the hard steel and observing by its deepening of color, the gradually lessening degrees of hardness. The term 'tempering' is often used to signify what really consists of the two very different processes of hardening and tempering.

"In selecting a medium for quenching the hot steel in hardening, it is our opinion that the workman will do well in general practice to confine himself to clear water at the temperature at which it flows from the ordinary sources of supply. An exception to this is in the hardening of very small pieces, such as single pivot drills, in which, for the sake of convenience, wax may be used. There are many nostrums in the shape of hardening mixtures, supposed by some to possess peculiar merits, but we have not heard of any cases in which such claims are supported by either theory or practical experience.

"A piece of steel after hardening will be found to be coated with a black oxide. For large work which requires subsequent dressing to size, etc., this is not a matter of importance; in hardening small work, however, it is desirable to prevent it by coating the article with moistened soap before heating. This melts over the steel and forms a protecting film; after quenching, the steel comes from the water with a silvery gray surface very easily polished preparatory to tempering. Any small portions of black scale happening to adhere can be removed with a steel or brass wire scratch brush or scraped

* The following explanation of hardening and tempering is from the book: "The Manipulation of Steel in Watch Work" by John J. Bowman:

off with a knife. In order to harden steel without discoloration or scaling of the metal, the object to be accomplished is simply the exclusion of air from the surface during heating and quenching.

"When one end only of a piece is to be hardened, do not plunge it to the end of the glowing portion and then let it rest until cool, but move it rapidly up and down, as otherwise the piece may be flawed or weakened at the part which was on a level with the surface of the water.

"For heating gravers to the desired color before quenching, the term "cherry red" is generally used, and we must say here that as there is a variance of color perception in the eyes of different persons, the same shade of color in the metal may appear differently, so the term used can be only approximate. To attain skill in hardening steel actual experience and much practice is necessary. Discussion of the subject is of course valuable, but there can be no absolute rules; one must learn by combining his own experience with what he may learn of others. Heat treating operations involving judging of colors may well be done always by the light from windows facing northward, which is most uniform under varying conditions of the weather, the time of day, and the seasons.

"Now we have come to the subject of tempering, or lessening, to suit our purpose, the degree of hardness the piece of steel has acquired from the heating and quenching. A fact which should be mentioned here is that steel will harden to different degrees by using metal containing different percentages of carbon; the more carbon the greater hardness with the same degree of heat. We believe manufacturers furnish steel of great uniformity for known purposes, such as the square rods used for making gravers, so that this 'percentage of carbon' question need not be considered in practical work.

"The same piece of steel may become very hard with great heat, and less so with a lower heat. In this matter of heating, experience must teach the happy medium between overheating and underheating. Always try your work for hardness with a file of rather fine cut. If underheated, the steel may come out of the quenching bath softer than it was before heating. Overheated or partially 'burnt' steel becomes coarse-grained and brittle. If not too far gone, it may be restored by heating to a good red and cooling slowly, but it will never again be fully as good as before.

"There are several methods of gauging the changes in the hardness of a piece of steel undergoing tempering. The two most generally used are (1) by observing the change in color of the steel, and (2) by noting the action of the heat on oil or tallow with which the steel is covered. It has been claimed that the oil method is the better, as being more certain than the color method because of the difference in color appreciation in the eyes of different persons. This opinion does not seem to take into consideration the fact that ignition and smoking will take place at different temperatures in different oils; the certainty of both methods would appear to be about equal, and as the color method is cleaner in operation and more convenient, we always favor it when possible."

The following table shows the various colors and temperatures in tempering steel.

Color	Temperature
1. Pale Straw	420° F.
2. Straw	450° F.
3. Yellow	480° F.
4. Brown	500° F.
5. Purple	530° F.
6. Bright Blue	580° F.
7. Deep Blue	590° F.
8. Light Blue with greenish tinge	640° F.

In this table, No. 1 is the temper generally used for gravers, although No. 2 and No. 3 will cut the softer metals. Any graver tempered as soft as to a brown color is of no use and must be rehardened and tempered.

Before proceeding to temper an article by color it is imperative that it, or at least a portion of it, be thoroughly clean. An emery stick of rather fine grain is good for the purpose. The cleaned surface must not be touched with the fingers nor anything greasy until after the coloring is finished. An alcohol lamp is convenient for drawing the temper. The procedure is illustrated in Fig. 46, step 5. Care must be taken to heat the heaviest part of the graver first, gradually moving back and forth through the flame toward the point so that when the first pale straw tint is observed, it will be uniform throughout the area heated.

Remove the steel from the heat as soon as the desired color is attained. In tempering large pieces, as soon as the color is reached, plunge into water, else the heat in the piece will carry the softening further than was intended.

2. Making a Square Graver

a. Filing and Shaping. To make good gravers only a few essential tools are needed: a jeweler's saw frame, saw blades, #2 and #4; hand files with handles, flat emery hand buffs #00, and a good grade of tool steel rod, ⅛ of an inch square.

Using the jeweler's saw requires delicate handling and considerable skill. The blade is adjusted by first tightening the screw controlling the length of the frame. Placing the saw blade in the upper clamp, tighten with the teeth pointing toward the lower clamp. Placing the upper end of the frame against the body of the operator, add a little pressure to the sawframe by bending the body forward and tighten the saw blade in the lower clamp. This provides tension, eliminating any "slack."

To start sawing, stroke the saw upward with light pressure. Two or three strokes will do and the regular sawing action may follow. The cutting is done on the downward stroke, and as the hand is pulled downward, add a little forward pressure. The upward stroke should receive no real pressure but should be allowed to slide lightly in position over the metal. A little beeswax applied to the blade will avoid jamming and prevent breakage.

Making gravers will not be the only use for the jeweler's saw. It will also become a necessary tool in sawing out inscription plates of a specific size (discussed in a later section).

To make a square graver, select a piece of steel stock ⅛ of an inch square. See Fig. 46, step 1. Mark off a 3¾ inch length and saw through diagonally, keeping in mind that this will be the 45-degree face angle when sharpening later. Clamp 2/3 of the graver length in a bench vise, leaving 1/3 of the length showing. File the graver to the shape indicated by step 2, Fig. 46, using a #2 file, then a #4 file and finally a #00 emery stick. In using the #2 file, the first strokes are made at right angles to the graver. After the shape is attained the file strokes may be run parallel with the length of the graver. This will smooth out all bumps and ridges and is called draw-filing. Continuing this stroke with the #4 file and #00 emery stick will result in a smoothly finished graver.

For those who are not adept at filing, the following excerpt adapted from the *Jewelry Repair Manual* by R. Allen Hardy will be helpful:

The best way to proceed in learning to file is to form a clear mental picture of what you are trying to do and how you must go about doing it. Filing is the gradual reduction of metal to a desired size and shape, using the simplest tool, the hand file.

The usual procedure in filing and shaping tools is first to rough it out to the approximate shape using coarse or rough files. Proceed cautiously so that too much metal is not filed away in any one spot. When the work becomes close to the correct size and shape, change to finer files. As the job is completed the finest files will leave a smooth surface.

To file a large piece of work, clamp it between the jaws of a vise attached to the work bench. Stand up to file. Hold the handle of the file in the right hand, the tip in the left. The right hand furnishes the push and power. The left hand guides the file and with a little pressure keeps it in constant contact with the metal being filed. As the finer files are used, a lighter stroke is needed.

Roughing out should be done quickly. For speedy filing the answer is in method, not muscle. Remember to file away corners as soon as they are formed. The first few strokes will leave flat surfaces. The edges of the flat spots will be the corners to file away. As corners are filed away, flat spots again appear but also more corners. The new corners present smaller cutting areas, so that the file will cut deeper and faster.

b. Hardening and Tempering. To harden, apply a thin film of dampened soap over the filed area (1/3 of the graver length). Holding the graver as shown in Fig. 46, step 3, direct the flame over the soaped area until the section is a cherry-red color. Then plunge the graver immediately into the water as shown in Fig. 46, step 4. In doing so, do not hold the graver motionless after plunging, but rather move it upward and downward until the metal has cooled. This will minimize the risk of warping or bending out of true.

Before tempering, the graver must be cleaned in order to correctly determine the color. Use a #00 emery stick to remove discoloration remaining from the hardening operation. Proceed, then, to temper the graver as shown in Fig. 46, step 5. The graver should be heated first at the beginning of the taper and gradually pulled through the flame as indicated by the arrow in the illustration. Do this slowly, moving the graver through the flame as many times as necessary to effect the color change. The first tinge of yellow or straw color should show at the thickest section of the taper and be gradually worked down or pulled out to the very tip of the graver. If the color appears to be darkening too rapidly, plunge the graver in water. Colors tend to continue to darken after the work is removed from the flame.

3. Correcting Defective Gravers

Gravers may be defective in many ways. The metal may be too hard or too soft, or it is possible the carbon may be "burnt out" of the graver rendering the tool useless, because further heat treatment will not restore it to its original condition.

If a graver is found to be hard or brittle, points break easily. Tempering the metal to a light straw will eliminate the brittleness, strengthen the point and improve cutting generally.

A graver that is too soft does not hold a point; this is not because the point breaks, but because it wears away. In some instances the point of a too-soft graver will bend over, showing a distinct burr. To correct this condition the entire procedure of hardening and tempering must be repeated.

Occasionally gravers are found that will not respond to hardening and tempering. Points continue to break, and often when sharpening, a good cutting edge will not appear. This condition indicates the carbon content of the steel is defective, "burnt out" or otherwise useless. The graver should be discarded.

4. Altering Gravers for Improved Cutting

Rarely does a square graver need an alteration, unless the engraver desires a particular shape and wishes to remodel the tool. Attention will be directed, here, to alterations that will occur in the following section, dealing with flat, round and lining gravers.

FIG. 47. To bend graver to the desired shape, heat area with a thin flame and press on a hard asbestos pad. Heat and bend gradually and avoid overheating. Be sure line of centers is kept straight. Graver may be held in pinvise during operation.

Round and lining gravers are not faced on the belly. To do so would remove the lines on the liner and the shape of the round graver would be spoiled. A problem of acquiring "lift" instantly arises on straight gravers. Curved liners and curved round gravers are sometimes available but are not so plentiful that the beginner may select any size he would like. Most liners and round gravers obtainable are straight, making it necessary for the beginner to heat and bend the tips as shown in Fig. 47. The metal must be rehardened and tempered in the usual manner.

In the event the engraver is fortunate enough to obtain curved liners and round gravers, alterations are still necessary but they do not include rehardening and tempering. Instead the curve is reduced by grinding on the India stone until the engraver reaches the degree of belly angle or lift satisfactory to his own wishes. More detail will be given this subject in the following section.

An important point to remember concerning square, round, flat or lining gravers is this: most trouble or difficulty in cutting arises from an incorrect belly angle. By grinding the correct belly angle on square and flat gravers, control of gravers can be thoroughly mastered. By patiently altering or bending the liners and round gravers the "happy medium" will be found, the tendency to slip will disappear and confidence greatly increased.

Chapter 7

Cutting Block Alphabets

1. Preparing and sharpening tools for cutting all types of block lettering: (a) flat tools; (b) round tools; (c) liners.
2. Drawing on paper. Plain Block Alphabet and numerals; principles of construction.
3. Cutting stems and bars squaring off ends with triangular shade cuts or "picks."
4. Cutting plain block alphabet and numerals.
5. Cutting names, dates, inscriptions.
6. Construction of Capped Block Alphabet; method of cutting.
7. Cutting names, dates, inscriptions.
8. Wriggling with flat tool.
9. Cutting with liner—names, dates, inscriptions.
10. Wriggling with liner.
11. Combination cutting using wriggle and bright cut, liner and flat tool, etc.
12. Drawing (on paper) Gothic Alphabet and Numerals for cutting with round tool; principles of construction.
13. Cutting Gothic Alphabet and Numerals.
14. Cutting names, dates, inscriptions.
15. Cutting large block letters for fill-in work and shading.

DESIGNING and cutting the following block alphabets involves engraving of a nature entirely different from the sections already covered. Script, Ribbon, and Vertical script may be considered the alphabets most artistic in appearance due to their oval or round shape and flowing lines.

Roman Block is the "in-between" alphabet in the program-outline, being cut with the square graver and with some letters having the same oval or round construction found in the preceding alphabets. At the same time, most of the letter formations are angular, thus placing it partially in the mechanical group of alphabets, in which category falls the simple block style to be studied next.

To further emphasize the contrast between the alphabets already covered and the ones to follow, it is entirely possible to construct all simple block alphabets with a ruler, using proportions measured exactly, leaving nothing whatever to the imagination. Those students who lean more to the mechanical side will find their aptitude for this style greatly increased; those who are more artistically inclined may find it dull and rather monotonous. A really good engraver, however, is judged by his overall ability and consistency, even though the mastery of script is of most importance.

The gravers used for the next phase of cutting are of varied shapes and sizes; the manipulation of the tools in cutting requires a different technique. The complete tool has a different "feel," due to the comparatively short graver handle and the exposed graver length. Heretofore, all cutting has been done with the finger tips well cushioned against a wooden graver handle. Now the "feel" is changed; the finger tips will not be cushioned at all, but will rest against the bare metal.

The response of the graver as cutting proceeds is not as fine and delicate as experienced with the square graver, where a sensitive "touch" is so important. Instead, due to the broadness of the cutting edge and the manner of cutting "flat," greater resistance is encountered, resulting in a different technique of control.

1. Preparing and Sharpening Tools

Gravers used for cutting block letters are referred to as flat gravers, round gravers and lining gravers, or liners. Their construction is decidedly different from the square graver with its adjustable handle. (See Figs. 48 to 53.) The gravers as they are manufactured are generally much too long. To correctly alter them, it is necessary to shorten them from the handle end, taking care to restore the original taper by shaping on a grinding stone. The wooden handles are drilled to receive the gravers, which are driven on by holding a graver securely in a vise, lightly tapping the handle with a hammer. The overall length of all such tools should be from 3¾ inches to 4½ inches. This may seem short but after working with them it will be

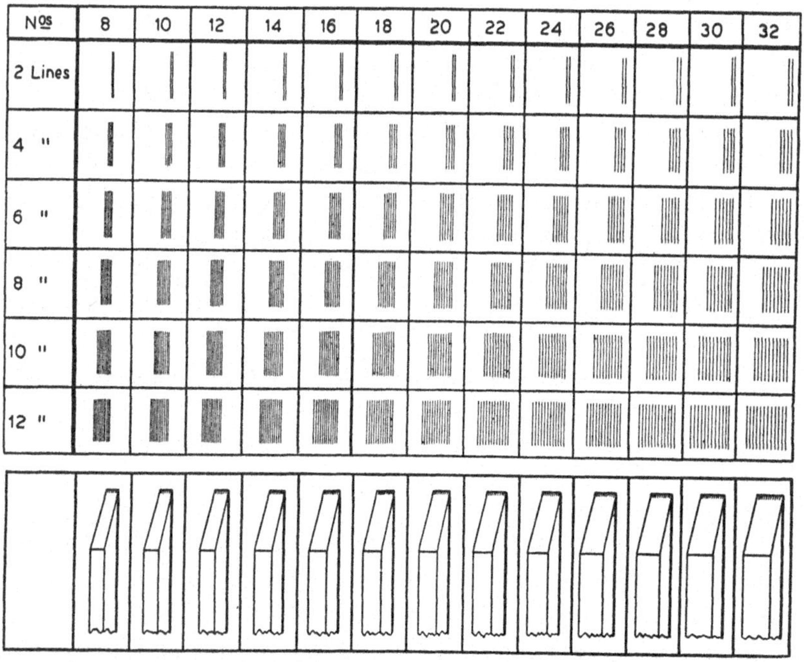

Nos	8	10	12	14	16	18	20	22	24	26	28	30	32
2 Lines													
4 "													
6 "													
8 "													
10 "													
12 "													

Fig. 48. Set of lining gravers from two to 12 lines in 13 sizes.

found that a short graver is more easily controlled. Long gravers are more inclined to slip.

Flat gravers, round gravers, and liners may be purchased in various sizes or widths. In acquiring a balanced selection the beginner should have at least the following sizes: Flat gravers, No. 36, No. 37, No. 38, No. 40, No. 42; round gravers, No. 50, No. 51, No. 52; liners, No. 8-4, No. 8-6, No. 8-8, No. 8-10. In selecting liners the first number denotes the number of the graver, the second denotes the number of lines on the graver. One other graver may be added to this group: a No. 1 knife-edge graver. This tool is converted into a small flat graver and will be discussed later in the text. In time more sizes may be added as the engraver sees fit, especially liners. A wide assortment of liners is highly desirable since the engraver is often called upon to duplicate or match engraving done by someone else.

The flat gravers may be sharpened first. The rear line of the

FIG. 49. Lining gravers (side view). Top, bent type; bottom, straight.

FIG. 50. Flat graver.

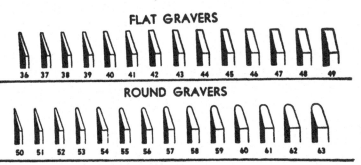

FIG. 51. Different sizes of flat and round gravers.

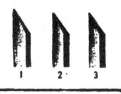

FIG. 52. Knife gravers.

FIG. 53. Flat side graver handle.

graver's belly must be straight and is shaped first, Fig. 54A. Then the face is done as shown in Fig. 54B and C. The result should be a perfectly straight cutting edge; a 45-degree face angle is correct. The belly angle should be slight. An extreme belly angle widens the cutting edge causing, for example, a No. 38 flat graver to become a No. 40 in cutting width.

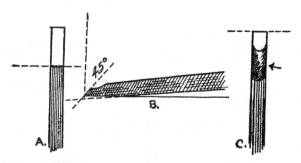

FIG. 54. Graver sharpening. In flat tools, sharpen belly first (A). Dotted line must be straight. Belly angle (B) should be slight. Face angle 45 degrees. Sharpen face last (C). Excess metal at arrow is ground away to make refacing easier.

To sharpen liners (Fig. 55), face them only, with a 45-degree face angle. Do not touch the belly. Burrs between lines may be removed by stabbing the point into a block of wood.

Round tools should be faced with a 45-degree face angle. See Fig. 56. Nothing should be done to the belly unless it happens to be

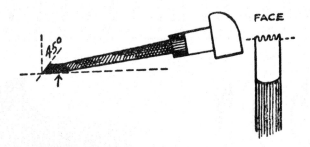

FIG. 55. Liners should have a 45 degree face angle. Lift should be added by softening tip and bending up at arrow. Reharden and draw to light straw color.

too rough and shows lines. In this case, it may be smoothed out on an Arkansas stone in a rolling motion to preserve the original roundness. Then it should be polished on emery paper.

Liners and round tools are sometimes available with curved ends. An extreme curve is useful for engraving extreme, concave surfaces, but hardly suitable for average work, having too much lift. Such a graver may be altered to use for average work by shortening the length from the cutting end. In doing so, the extreme curve may be greatly reduced leaving a slight curve, with a desired 8 to 12-degree belly angle.

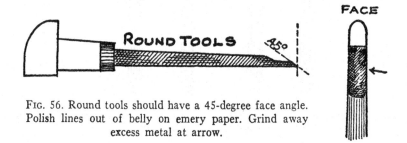

FIG. 56. Round tools should have a 45-degree face angle. Polish lines out of belly on emery paper. Grind away excess metal at arrow.

Straight liners and round tools have a tendency to cut deep. Since the belly is not ground on the stone, the only way to arrive at a belly angle is to bend the tips of the gravers enough to compensate for the belly angle naturally acquired in sharpening square and flat gravers. This may be done by placing the tip of the graver on an asbestos pad and with a flame gradually heat the area until the graver tip will bend under slight pressure. See Fig. 55 at arrow. After completing this operation, the graver must be rehardened and tempered to a light straw color.

Figs. 54 and 56 show a hollowed-out section (indicated by arrow) on top of the graver near the point. This metal is ground away for two distinct reasons. The operation reduces the size of the face, saving time when resharpening; a small area of metal being more quickly ground away than a large area. Reducing the size of the tip of the graver results also in a more sensitive tool, one that is easier to control when cutting.

Fig. 57 illustrates some common errors in sharpening flat gravers or liners. (1) and (2) show incorrect belly lines resulting from tilting the graver too far over to one side when using the sharpener. (3) and (4) show an incorrect face which can result either from tilting the graver too far over to one side or by neglecting to correct an error in shaping of the belly.

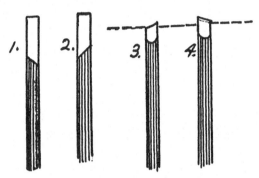

FIG. 57. Common errors. (1) Incorrect belly line. (2) Incorrect belly line. (3) Incorrect face. (4) Incorrect face.

2. Drawing on Paper

Design on paper the plain block alphabet and numerals as shown in Fig. 58. Use letters ¾ of an inch in height. This alphabet can be mechanically constructed. Each letter should be the same width with the exception of the "M" and "W." These two letters can be made a trifle wider since they have four stems. The numbers are also the same width. In constructing the corners, be sure all corresponding corners are parallel, and by all means the same in length of cut. The bars are made one-half the length of the stems.

3. Cutting Stems and Bars

A careful study of Fig. 59A-A' will help to form a clear conception of what is wanted in flat graver cutting. A shows a correct flat graver cut of uniform depth (cross-section). A' shows the same cut, top view. Fig. 59D shows an incorrect flat graver cut (cross-section). One side is cutting deeper. For uniform depth the graver must be sharpened correctly and must not be tilted to one side when executing the cut. D' shows the same cut, top view.

Lay out a series of parallel perpendicular lines about ¼ of an inch in height on a practice plate. With a No. 38 flat graver, cut

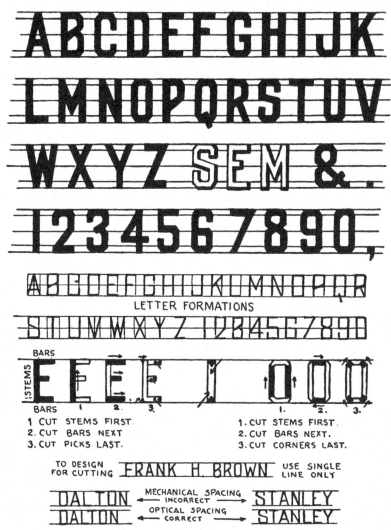

Fig. 58. Block alphabet mechanically constructed on paper.

these lines and square off the ends with a triangular pick using a script graver or a No. 40 flat graver. Direction of cutting a pick is shown in the lower center of Fig. 58. These picks are most important because when placed crooked, too high or too low, the letter becomes distorted. Much practice is necessary because the handling of the tool is so different from the script graver. It will be found in the beginning that a straight line is difficult to execute. The graver

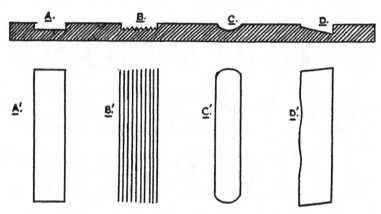

FIG. 59. Top and cross-section views of graver and liner cuts.

may want to pull to the right or the left. If the cutting edge is perfectly straight, this tendency will be minimized. Try to get evenness of depth in cut. A common error is to cut deeper on one side. This will pull the cut out of line and interfere with proper control.

4. Cutting Plain Block Alphabet and Numerals

In designing, preliminary to cutting, it is not necessary to use a double line for each cut placement. On the contrary, a single line is more desirable. See Fig. 58. The letter "E" should be designed as shown in the "letter formations" and cut in the order shown by steps 1, 2, and 3, under the large letter "E." To cut the stem, the graver may be placed directly over the vertical line. The top bar may be cut with the graver following the lower edge of the line. The bar at the bottom of the letter is cut with the graver following

FIG. 60. Flat plates are used for practice in cutting inscriptions.

the top edge of the line. The center bar may be cut by placing the graver directly over the line. The order of cutting letters having corners is shown in Fig. 58, steps 1, 2, and 3 under the letter "O."

In cutting the alphabet, first cut all letters that are without corners. This involves straight stems and bars which are squared-off alike. When a corner is formed as at the bottom of the "E," a full pick is not made (see Fig. 58, lower left), but a very small pick is used coming in from the same angle as in cutting a Roman serif. The corner only needs to be accentuated, not squared-off. Next, cut the letters with corners. All stems and bars are cut first, the corners last. After cutting the alphabet, the cutting of numbers presents no further problem.

5. Cutting Names, Dates, Inscriptions

As in Chapter 5, item 5, follow the same procedure in cutting names, dates, and inscriptions. Starting with the No. 38 graver, gradually reduce the size of the graver as smaller letters are cut. The smallest flat graver used is made from the No. 1 knife edge tool. The belly can be faced to the desired width (2/3 the width of a No. 36 graver). Practical work on a flat plate would be a name and date cut with gravers No. 38, No. 37 and No. 36, in that order; a four or five line inscription with the No. 38 and No. 36 combined. Use the No. 38 flat graver for the principal lines and the No. 36 for the least important lines, a good rule to follow. The designed layout for such inscriptions is illustrated in Fig. 60.

In laying out and cutting a small five-line inscription using the No. 1 knife-edge (altered to flat), or No. 36 flat tool, it is best to design all lines the same size. If emphasis is wanted on one or more lines the first letters of words appearing on these lines may be made slightly taller.

6. Construction of Capped Block Alphabet

The capped block alphabet has the same basic construction as simple block with the addition of caps rather than picks to square off ends. See Fig. 61 for design and method of cutting. Bars are

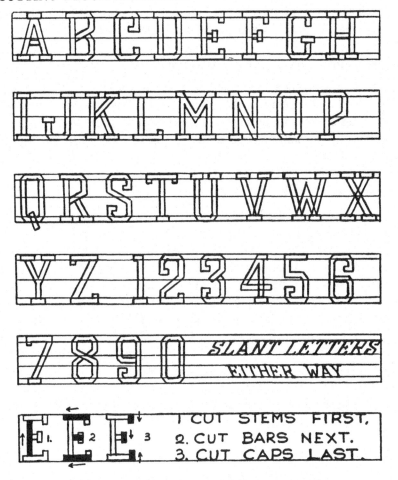

FIG. 61. Capped block alphabet.

extended to form half-caps over the tops and bottoms of stems such as on the letter "E." Caps are made in one cut.

7. Cutting Names, Dates, Inscriptions

Using the capped block alphabet, follow the same procedure as explained under item 5 of this section. A difference in spacing capped block letters will be noticed on the first word attempted. The caps take up more room and spacing letters is similar to spacing Roman style letters.

8. Wriggling with Flat Tool

Beginning with the No. 38 flat tool, practice the wriggle cut using straight lines. The technique is shown in Fig. 62 A, B, C, D, E, and F. To wriggle, the graver should be held higher than usual and rocked back and forth from corner to corner. When properly executed, a steady rhythmic bump will be felt as each point rocks back and forth. Experience must be gained before a straight wriggled line results. For practice work, names and dates can be done with the No. 38 tool. Then try the No. 42 and No. 40 gravers. Due to the increase in width, the height of the letters must be greatly increased and the student must be cautioned to design slimmer letters. The length of the bar should be reduced to about 1/3 of the stem length. On the large tool cuts, the ends are squared off with tiny serifs, since it is impossible to make picks this large.

9. Cutting with Liners

With the liners, follow the same procedure as explained under item 5 of this section. It will be noted that liners have a tendency to leave trails, but this can be overcome by bending the tips slightly upward to add lift to the gravers. (Explained under item 1, this section.) Care must be taken that the tool is not bent to the right or left, as this would throw it out of line and cause trouble in cutting. Fig. 59B and B' show the cross-section and top view of a liner cut.

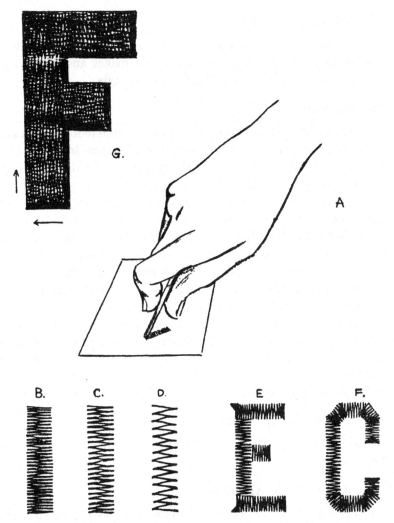

FIG. 62. The Wriggle Cut. (A) To wriggle, raise hand and arm, rock graver back and forth. (B) Fine wriggle, not adaptable to soft metals. (C) Medium wriggle, best for average single-cut lettering. (D) Coarse wriggle, not for single-cut lettering. (E), (F) Square off tips with triangular picks. (G) Example of cross-wriggle.

10. Wriggling with Liners

With the large liners, try wriggling in the same manner as explained under item 8 of this section. This makes an attractive cut and is more acceptable than the flat tool wriggle.

11. Combination Cutting

Combination cutting is done by using two different width gravers with contrasting cuts. For example, design a name in simple block style. Cut the stems with a No. 38 flat graver and the bars with a No. 36, straight- or bright-cut. The result will be attractive. Liners can be used for the stems and a narrow flat graver for the bars. Cut a name using this combination. Another interesting effect is to use the wide flat tool wriggle for the stems and a narrow flat tool bright-cut for the bars; square off ends with regular Roman serifs. Cut a name of this type. If undecided which lines to cut thick and which to cut thin as on the letters "N-A-V," refer to the Roman alphabet. The location of contrasting thicknesses is the same.

Many different and interesting effects can be worked out using two different size gravers. The reader should experiment with the idea. It will be found that strong Roman letters can be made by using a wide flat graver for the stems, a thin flat graver for the bars and a script graver to execute the curved portions of the letters.

12. Drawing Gothic Alphabet

Design on paper the Gothic alphabet and numerals. See Fig. 63 for construction.

13. Cutting Gothic Alphabet

In cutting the Gothic letters, all stems must have an up-cut and a returning down-cut to insure the same width from top to bottom. See Fig. 63, steps 1 to 12. There is a tendency of this graver to cut shallow at the beginning of the cut, resulting in a taper before getting into the true width. Hence, a back-cut is necessary. See Fig. 59C and C' for cross-section and top view. The curved letters cannot receive a back-cut since the cutting would have to be done clockwise. If the curved cut does not match the width of the straight stems, simply over-cut to insure uniform width of line. The straight cuts are comparatively easy to make. More practice is needed on the curved letters because the curvature must always be perfectly regular. When the cuts are mastered, design and cut the alphabet and numerals using the No. 52 graver.

ABCDEFGHI
JKLMNOPQR
STUVWXYZ
1234567890

FIG. 63. Gothic alphabet for round tool. (1) Cut up on stems. (2) Back cut same line. (3) Finished stem. (4) Cut to left on bar. (5) Back cut same line. (6) Finished line. (7) Stems and bars cut. (8) Stems and bars back cut. (9) Finished letter. (10) Cut to left on curves. (11) Back cut tip only. (12) Finished letter. Curved lines may be overcut to obtain correct width of line. Do not back cut.

14. Cutting Names, Dates, Inscriptions

Follow the usual procedure in cutting names, dates, and inscriptions as explained under item 5 of this section. Begin with the larger gravers, gradually reducing the size until the small No. 50 can be handled equally as well as the No. 52.

15. Cutting for Fill-in Work

Filling-in and shading large block letters (Fig. 64) is really a build-up to the treatment of block monograms. Carefully work these out. First design the letter, hairline the outline, fill in the letter, then shade the lower right portion.

The proper shading of the letter is usually confusing, so the point will be cleared up now. The heavy shade lines are placed outside of the filled-in design. The cut is never placed inside the stem proper for an obvious reason. This would decrease the width and weaken the effect. The shades would be just as correct if placed at the upper left, lower left, or upper right of the letter, but generally they are placed at the lower right, so all work will be done using this system to avoid confusion.

The number of usable fill-ins are too numerous to mention here. Only the most practical and popular types will be discussed. First and best is cross-lining. This is done by laying-out a series of diagonal lines across the designed letter. (Fig. 64, the letter "E.") Then, cut closely spaced hairlines starting at the left, cutting diagonally up to the right. Be sure to begin each cut at the hair-lined edge of the letter and finish the cut by cutting into the opposite hair-lined edge. By cutting into the hairline, no burrs or unfinished cuts are made. There is an increased probability of making a few light slips, but these will be eliminated by the heavy shade line on the right of the stem. Care must be taken to keep all crosslines parallel. Different effects may be obtained by using slightly shaded crosslines with lines spaced a little wider apart. Crosslines may also be laid out horizontally or diagonally, slanting the opposite way.

Another widely used fill-in is called matting or cross-wriggling with a liner. (See Fig. 62G, Fig. 64, the letter "H.") The

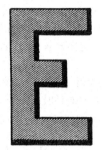

Cross-lined
and shaded.

Cross wriggle
with liner.

Picked with
round tool.

Roman cross-lined and off-shaded.

Ribbon cut

Horizontal crossline

Vertical lining

FIG. 64. Fill-ins for letters and monograms.

letter-effect is regular and does not look like a wriggle-cut at all when done properly. To do this, make vertical, wriggled lines with a wide liner, filling in the entire letter. Then make a series of horizontal wriggles directly across the others.

Another solid fill-in consists of a series of round picks placed close together using a large round graver. (Fig. 64, the Old English "T.") All picks should be made from the same direction, as any change will show a different reflection of light.

A very satisfactory method of shading a letter is to place the shade cuts all around the letter instead of just the lower right. See Fig. 64, the letter "R." Two methods are used in executing these shadings. A single wide shade line is used, or three or four light ribbon cuts, depending on the width of shade desired. Both methods should be practiced as they are of equal importance. Another way is to add an off-shaded hairline. See Fig. 64, the "N. R. G." on the plaque. This is always placed parallel to the heavy shade. The shade and off-shade must show a slight space between the two cuts.

Single letters using these fill-ins can well be used where a large letter is desired as on a belt buckle.

Chapter 8

Cutting Old English Alphabet

---

1. Drawing on paper; principles of construction.
2. Cutting alphabet and numerals; using (a) flat tool (wriggle and bright cut); (b) liner (wriggle and straight cut).
3. Cutting names, dates, inscriptions.
4. Cutting large Old English for fill-in work using (a) ribbon cut; (b) cross-lining; (c) fancy cuts.

OLD ENGLISH is a highly acceptable alphabet much in demand. Although the average layman is sometimes confused in determining what certain letters are, the alphabet style is easily recognized in a number of varied forms.

At first glance, the alphabet appears completely artistic, complicated and possibly very confusing. In reality only the effect is artistic; the letters themselves follow exact mechanical principles of construction. As the learner proceeds, the simplicity of the design will become apparent.

The Old English style has many variations, some with considerable beauty and simplicity, some with extremely complicated formations, not conducive to easy reading. In presenting a suitable style for instruction, a simple form, clear cut and easily legible was chosen. From a knowledge of this alphabet the more complicated forms should hold no serious problem.

1. Drawing Old English Alphabet and Numerals

The Old English alphabet has a simple system of construction. See Fig. 65, lower left, for the designing. The key consists of three lines, one vertical and two diagonals. The stems are up-cuts, and are all parallel to the vertical lines. The diagonal joints or corners are all parallel to one diagonal line. The hair-line connections are all parallel to the other diagonal line.

Naturally, a few odd cuts will appear that have no relation at all to the key. They should not be confusing since they are so obviously different. For example, the top cut of the capital "D" is horizontal and appears in no other letter. The top of the "T" and the center of

FIG. 65. Old English alphabet.

the "Z" are individual double-cuts and are not comparable to other cuts. The small curved cuts or flags that branch from the left of the upright stems of the capital letters are out of line with the Old English key and may be treated individually. They are located horizontally. There are three such curved cuts that appear throughout the Old English alphabet; the center flag, just discussed, the top flag as appearing just above the left stem of the letter "B," and the lower flag appearing at the base of the letter "B." The cuts should be studied, one in relation to the other two. The center flag is always the smallest, the top flag always slightly larger, and the lower flag considerably the largest of the three. The proportionate sizes will be noted by studying the Old English alphabet shown in the illustration.

In designing the lower case alphabet fewer variations from the key will be found. Most letters are made up of straight cuts.

The numbers are consistent in design, with horizontal lines appearing in the "2," "4," "5," and "7."

2. Cutting Old English Alphabet and Numerals

To cut the Old English alphabet, the same gravers are used as in block lettering. The flat graver and liner can be used with a straight cut or wriggle. First consider the No. 38 flat graver. Make a plate of the alphabet; capitals, lower case, and numbers, using a bright cut. The only new cut to learn is how to make a slight curve with a flat graver. All short curves are more easily handled with a flat graver while the long extreme curves as found in the letter "S" are best handled with a square graver. The outer edge of the curved cuts can be hair-lined. In making hair-line connections, taking the lower case "o" for example, the hair-line should be slightly curved so that the end of each broad line is squared-off without leaving a gap. Any gaps occurring in making these connections can be closed with a light cut using a square graver. Always check the cuts for gaps. They cause an unsightly appearance on otherwise good work.

3. Cutting Names, Dates, Inscriptions

Cut names, dates, and inscriptions using all flat gravers except the No. 40 and No. 42. Use the flat tool and liner, straight cut and wriggle.

A liner presents a special problem. The straight cuts are easily executed but the curved cuts demand a lot of practice, so it is advisable to practice only on the curved letters before attempting names, etc. In cutting the letter "C," the curve is made by starting with one point of the liner, gradually laying over the graver until its greatest width is reached, then tapering back to the one point. The principle is the same as in cutting a script shade line. Trim this cut with a light hair-line and complete the full curve of the letter "C." All curved lines are handled in the same manner.

To wriggle a curved cut in Old English, the reader will find it easy to wriggle-in the greatest width of a stem with the flat graver or liner and form the taper at either end with a square graver. A single tapered shade cut, or two or three light ribbon cuts may be used, depending on the width of the wriggle. Great pains must be taken with connections or the effect is apt to be choppy. The straight wriggle-cuts present no new problem.

4. Cutting for Fill-in Work

Old English may be filled-in and shaded in the same manner as explained in Chapter 7, item 15. Design and cut a name and date using cross-line for filling-in. The correct shading can be found in Fig. 65, lower right. The one shading problem peculiar to Old English is deciding where to shade the curved developments or flags. To do this successfully, think in terms of left and right. The flags developing to the right are shaded on the top side; the flags developing to the left are shaded underneath. The letter "T" (Fig. 65, lower right) has an unusual curved top. Shading is placed partly underneath and partly on top.

Design and cut a name and date, using four ribbon cuts. The straight lines are cut with three upward strokes and one downward stroke as explained in cutting the Roman alphabet. Naturally this type of cutting is done only on large letters, so be sure to design the letters large enough and the stems thick enough for the fill-in to show up. The curved cuts are treated in the same manner as any ribbon-type formation, all running in the same direction.

Design and cut several Old English capitals, using the various fill-ins as learned in Chapter 7, item 15.

Chapter 9

Designing and Cutting Monograms

1. Construction and designing.
2. Special shadings.
3. Designing diamond monograms.
4. Cutting diamond monograms.
5. Designing round monograms.
6. Cutting round monograms: (a) block; (b) ribbon.
7. Designing square monograms.
8. Cutting square monograms.
9. Designing fancy monograms.
10. Cutting fancy monograms.

THE SUBJECT of monograms could well be treated as a completely separate operation in itself. Certainly there are enough different kinds and styles to make the prospective engraver dubious over the outlook of mastering all of them. Recently there has been little need for the engraver to concern himself with the ultra-elaborate designs popular early in his century. However, with today's nostalgic styles in clothing and jewelry, the hand engraver is in an excellent position to enhance his reputation (and pocketbook) by showing the more elaborate designs. Customers appreciate hand work and are willing to pay for it.

The monograms most in demand today are easily read, usually simple in construction, with the exception of the ribbon monogram or cipher. This latter type, while not necessarily nor deliberately complicated in design, usually works itself into an intricate arrangement due to the necessity of artistically weaving the letters together. Even so, the safest treatment to use is the simplest, and the ornate or elaborate effects should not be attempted without special instruction from the customer.

The block form of monograms may take countless, interesting shapes; sometimes plain, sometimes cleverly interlocked. An artistic touch is an asset, but hardly essential for the monograms of this nature because every line, curved or straight, may be mechanically constructed with pencil, ruler, and compass.

No attempt is made in this book to cover too wide a range of styles. It is much less confusing and certainly more instructive to the prospective engraver to dwell mainly on the practical monograms and concentrate on difficult phases of designing. From the basic and fundamental construction learned under this subject the beginner can be expected to develop his own ability and increase his ingenuity and foresight. However, there are books available containing a wealth of designs for the inspiration and example of engravers, both amateur and professional craftsmen, that have value much above what they cost. A good one is *Art Monograms and Lettering*, by J. M. Bergling, obtainable from jewelers' supplies dealers, whose businesses or branch stores are located in practically all large cities in the U.S.A.

1. Construction and Designing

Monograms are constructed in a variety of shapes and designs. It is in this phase of engraving that artistic ability is especially helpful and the designer will find an unlimited field for developing new ideas and letter treatments. Strange as it may seem, the block-type can be constructed mechanically with the use of a ruler and compass, depending not at all upon free-hand sketching for artistic effect. Even so, the idea is the thing, and the success of the monogram depends on the ingenuity and imagination of the designer.

Fig. 66 shows a group of monograms all different in shape and construction. It is not necessary to point out step by step how each line was placed; each monogram with its blocking-in or construction lines is self-explanatory.

2. Special Shadings

Special shadings and letter fill-ins are discussed in detail in Chapter 7, item 15. Since Fig. 66 deals primarily with monogram construction and not cutting, it will be necessary from time to time to refer to the illustration connected with Chapter 7, item 15. These illustrations explain cutting as well as design.

a. Cross-Shading or cross-lining, as it is also commonly called, is illustrated in Fig. 64—the letter "E." This type of fill-in has always

FIG. 66. Variations of monogram styles.

been and will continue to be the most desirable, especially on expensive articles.

b. Off-Shading a letter or monogram means to place the shade considerably away from the letter proper, creating a space between the letter and off-shade cut. The usual shaded letter or monogram has shade lines placed closely against the letter stems creating a more solid appearance. In Fig. 64, the letters "N-R-G," the off-shade is a hair-line placed to the right of all thick sections of the letter.

c. Hair-Line Shading, sometimes called ribbon shading, is simple enough to do and is used to good advantage especially on hard metals. The hair-lines are placed very close together, using as many cuts as are necessary to obtain the desired width. In using hair-line shades, the letters of the monogram may be shaded on the lower right or on all sides. This shading can be used with any type of letter fill-in. See Fig. 64, the letter "R" for an example.

d. Bright-Cut Shading is a term used to distinguish itself from hair-line shading. It requires only one wide shade line, placed solidly against the lower right sections of the filled-in letters, or it can be used on all sides.

e. Outlining a monogram or letter depends entirely on the shade placement to show off the letter. In this type of design the letters of the monogram are not filled-in; only the shades are placed. The most interesting effect is gotten when the letter is shaded only on the lower right. The rest of the letter receives no attention at all and the design, though unusual in appearance, is quite easy to read. A more definite result is gained by running the outline completely around the letters.

f. Relief monograms are designed in the usual manner with the addition of a line running completely around the monogram and parallel to its sides. The monogram may be round, square, oblong or any odd shape. If round, simply construct an additional circle spaced slightly away from the letters. Instead of filling-in the letters, fill-in the background around the letters. Shade the letters in the usual manner; shade also the border of the monogram; the result is a monogram in relief. In this manner, an effect of raised letters is obtained.

3. Designing Diamond Monograms

See Fig. 67 for accurate designing of diamond monograms. The novice engraver must familiarize himself with all letters in all positions by designing many monograms on paper before any cutting

FIG. 67. Each letter of the alphabet in three positions in diamond monograms.

is tried. Constructional lay-out of a diamond monogram is shown in Fig. 66, upper left corner.

4. Cutting Diamond Monograms

Select four of the best diamond monograms already designed. Fill-in the first with crosslining and shade all around each letter with a single shade cut. Monograms should measure about one inch across. On the second monogram lay-out a diamond border around the original design. Fill-in the background with crosslining and shade all around with ribbon cuts. On the third monogram, use the cross-wriggle fill-in done with a liner (Fig. 64H); shade all around with ribbon cuts, or a single shade line. Reduce the size of the fourth monogram to signet ring size. This will be about ½ inch across. Do not fill-in the letters but shade them all around with a prominent single shade line.

5. Designing Round Monograms

Design on paper round block monograms. Construction will be found in Fig. 66, upper right corner. Fig. 68 shows each letter of the alphabet in every position.

6. Cutting Round monograms

a. Block—select and cut four round monograms. Crossline the background of the first, shade the letters all around. Do not fill-in the letters. On the second monogram, cross-wriggle the background with a liner, bright-cut the letters all around. These monograms should measure about one inch to 1⅛ inch diameter. Reduce the third monogram to ¾ inch in diameter, fill-in the first letter with diagonal crosslining, slanting up toward center. Crossline the center letter with horizontal lines. Crossline the right letter with lines slanting down from center. The fourth monogram can be reduced to signet ring size, filled-in with a round tool pick, and shaded with a single shade cut.

b. Ribbon Monograms need special attention in designing. The formations of the different letters in different combinations is so varied that a complete study of all of them would become much

too involved. Instead a new approach to the subject will be made
with emphasis on simplicity of treatment. Refer to Fig. 69 for ideas
on how the monograms should look when complete. Here is shown
basic treatment of the two important stems by looping to the right
and to the left. The student should design these and so become completely familiar with the formations before attempting a monogram.

To begin the first monograms, use the combination "S-I-T" in
different positions; "I-T-S" and "T-S-I." The three letters are the

FIG. 68. Letters in each position in round block monograms.

simplest and will fall together with little effort. Make loops full and
round. Be sure stems curve continuously. Then, try other simple
combinations such as "O-P-Y" in different letter positions. After
skill and confidence have been built up on these, attempt the more
complicated combinations such as "B-R-M," "N-D-E," "W-H-Q,"
etc. Become familiar with letters that are similar in construction.
They can be grouped. Group No. 1—"A-H-K-M-N-U-V-W-X"—
consists of vertical stems. Group No. 2—"C-E-G-O-Q"—are simple

FIG. 68. Round block monograms, Continued.

oval constructions. Group No. 3—"B-D-F-L-I-J-P-R-S-T-Y-Z"—contain stem and oval combinations. The "D-L and Q" have peculiar constructions at the bottom and can create quite a problem when fitted in with other letters. Study Fig. 70 to get this letter treatment. Fig. 70 shows each letter of the alphabet in every position. In using these suggested letter arrangements, remember that in combining letters the formations may not work out exactly as illustrated in the figure; some slight alteration is invariably necessary.

FIG. 69. Ribbon monograms showing basic treatment of two important stems.

There are so many systems on how to design ribbon monograms that it is no wonder the beginner becomes confused and sometimes discouraged with this all-important phase of engraving. Having given several systems a fair trial and noting the confusion they create, this conclusion has been drawn. The simplest way to get designing results is *not to cross important stems* but to design the stems of each letter slim and apart from each other, using the outside loop of the letters to connect. This produces an airy monogram,

FIG. 70. Ribbon monograms with each letter shown in each of three positions.

easily read and definitely not crowded. The crossing of stems and over-exaggeration of fundamental loops if done properly and artistically produce interesting results and must not be considered incorrect. It requires more skill and aptitude than the average beginner has developed so far. Gratifying results have been achieved by inexperienced engravers using the suggested system.

When designing a given monogram, a valuable tip is to lay out, on paper, five circles 1½ inches in diameter. In the first circle, place the three letters at random letting loops fall where they naturally should. Study the letters and begin another design in the second circle. Here, an attempt can be made to loop the letters symmetrically. If the result is not quite satisfactory start another design in circle No. 3. Do not erase or touch-up anything in No. 2. By studying No. 2, considerable improvement can be made in No. 3. If not yet satisfactory, try again in No. 4. Following this method, a satisfactory monogram may be reached in circle No. 5. The great advantage is in having all of the attempts before you and so improving step by step.

Select and cut the four best monograms. The first should measure 1½ inches in diameter; the second 1⅛ inches; the third ¾ inches; the fourth ½ inch or signet ring size. It will be found that a good design leads to good cutting and a poor design to poor cutting.

7. Designing Square Monograms

Design, in block lettering, square monograms. No special explanation of the technique is required for this type design. The letters are placed side by side forming a square.

8. Cutting Square Monograms

Cut one monogram 7/8 inch square. Cut another 1/2 inch square. This last is just right for modern signet rings.

9. Designing Fancy Monograms

Fancy monograms may include any monogram whose design departs from the usual diamond, round, or square shape. Fig. 66 shows many monograms of this nature with their original construction lines. Design one each of the suggested monograms, preparatory to cutting.

10. Cutting Fancy Monograms

Cut the fancy monograms designed under item 9, choosing fill-ins that harmonize with the particular monogram shape. For example, the monogram "P-A-E" (Fig. 66) suggests two fill-ins, one for the letter "E," and one for the smaller letters "P-A." When two fill-ins are used in the same monogram, contrast is necessary. The "P-A" fill-in might well be crosslined to go with the cross-wriggle liner fill-in for the letter "E." This technique is permissible on all monograms where one letter is greatly emphasized. Monograms like the "S-R-G," "R-D-N," and "B-C-H" (Fig. 66) are more effective when only one fill-in is used.

Chapter 10

Final General Instructions

---

1. Designing and layout on the work; judging place for engraving; choosing styles of engraving for inscriptions and ornamental or decorative work as applied to (a) bracelets (identification type); (b) bracelets (round, solid type); (c) loving cups; (d) baby cups; (e) pitchers, bowls; (f) watch cases; (g) casket plates; (h) inside ring engraving.
2. Cementing work too small to be held by block attachments.
3. Transferring designs for engraving silver flatware.
4. Duplicating signatures.
5. Designing and cutting emblems.
6. Cutting for fill-in work on celluloid, pyralin and other plastic wares.
7. Making inscription plates, brass or other metals: (a) preparation; (b) engraving; (c) oxidizing; (d) lacquering.
8. Designing and engraving comprehensive sample plate.

THE FINAL SECTION of this book is of major importance, not being merely as a review of all that has gone before, but introducing new methods and procedures of cutting especially adapted to curved surfaces. In some instances new alphabets are suggested to facilitate cutting especially difficult surfaces.

This section will include the practical work that the finished engraver may expect to encounter the moment he first starts seriously practicing the art. Of course, there will be problems of engraving to which no reference has been made in the text. The articles and surfaces chosen for instruction here were especially selected either because they are exactly what will be encountered or because the particular surface is the same as found on many different articles.

The technique for cutting curved surfaces must be developed carefully. Immediate success is hardly to be expected. Whatever confidence the beginner has acquired up to this point can easily be lost unless it is realized that here is a new phase of work, requiring the utmost care and perseverance. When fear of curved surfaces is overcome the reader has arrived, so to speak, at a desirable peak of accomplishment.

1. Designing and Layout on the Work

This final section will not only put to practical use all that has so far been learned but will also stress the importance of laying out the design in the correct proportionate size to the article being engraved. In entering a general discussion of the subject one of the main points to remember is this: engraving on most articles should appear small and neat. Engraving a large design in a small space usually results in a poor appearance, however well it may be cut.

There are some articles that demand a large design in a small space but the reason is usually obvious. For example, some cigarette lighters present a very small space for engraving and the design should be done quite large, proportionately, else the engraving will not show up at all. Monograms demand more size than three initials in the same given space; example, a ribbon monogram on the back of a watch may cover 2/3 to 3/4 the entire area while the same letters, designed as three straight initials, follow the usual role of small, neat letters. See Fig. 71 for ideas on proportionate sizes.

In selecting articles to give the beginner a well-rounded background preparatory to practical work, only those items that require special study and handling were chosen. If instruction is followed closely, articles not mentioned here will be found, in most cases, to be similar or identical to articles included in the program of study. For example, flatware has been selected as a very important subject and is dealt with in detail. After completing flatware, the handling and cutting of a small pen-knife is no problem since the surface and the method of clamping in the block is about the same. Many articles would be treated in much the same manner, so detailed reference to each and every one is not necessary.

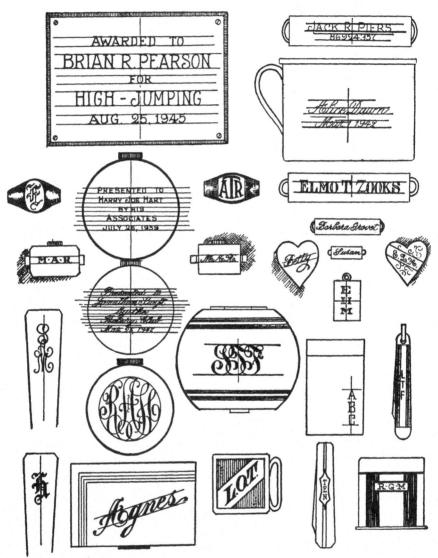

FIG. 71. Laying out practical work—style and size.

Before beginning to cut on curved surfaces, study Fig. 72. Shown here are differently shaped curved gravers which greatly aid the engraver in cutting different surfaces. Although some of them (such as the extreme curves for inside bowl engraving) are not too frequently used, it is quite impossible to engrave in the bottom of a bowl with any other type.

While curved gravers used for inside ring engraving and for open concave surfaces (such as the backs of bracelets) are very handy and simplify the cutting considerably, the beginner is urged

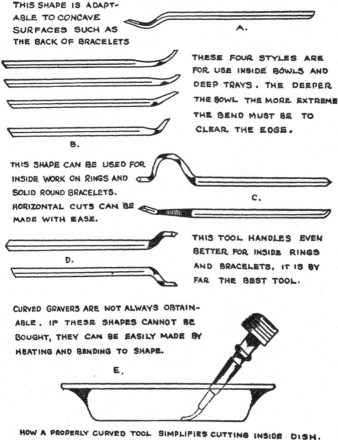

THIS SHAPE IS ADAPTABLE TO CONCAVE SURFACES SUCH AS THE BACK OF BRACELETS

A.

THESE FOUR STYLES ARE FOR USE INSIDE BOWLS AND DEEP TRAYS. THE DEEPER THE BOWL THE MORE EXTREME THE BEND MUST BE TO CLEAR THE EDGE.

B.

THIS SHAPE CAN BE USED FOR INSIDE WORK ON RINGS AND SOLID ROUND BRACELETS. HORIZONTAL CUTS CAN BE MADE WITH EASE.

C.

THIS TOOL HANDLES EVEN BETTER FOR INSIDE RINGS AND BRACELETS. IT IS BY FAR THE BEST TOOL.

D.

CURVED GRAVERS ARE NOT ALWAYS OBTAINABLE. IF THESE SHAPES CANNOT BE BOUGHT, THEY CAN BE EASILY MADE BY HEATING AND BENDING TO SHAPE.

E.

HOW A PROPERLY CURVED TOOL SIMPLIFIES CUTTING INSIDE DISH.

FIG. 72. Useful curved tools.

to try this type of cutting without the use of the curved tool. This will develop skill to a greater degree. Many experienced engravers never resort to a curved tool for inside ring work or concave bracelet work.

Cut off five lengths of copper from an average practice plate using a width of 3/8 to 1/2 an inch. Use the width of the plate for the length of the bracelet. Curve to simulate an identification bracelet. Referring to Fig. 71 for proportionate size, design and cut on the front:

1. Name and serial number—Gothic lettering, using round graver.
2. Name and serial number—Block lettering, using flat graver. Use capped block.
3. Name and serial number—Block lettering, using liner. Use picked block.
4. Name—Roman lettering.
5. Name—Script lettering.

Fig. 73 shows how the bracelet is held in the block.

Curved surfaces present a different problem in cutting. It will be found that by increasing the lifts, especially on a script tool, the cutting will go easier. The student can best determine for himself how great a degree of lift is required. First attempts at curved surface cutting may prove disheartening, but arriving at the correct lift will produce immediate and satisfying results.

Design and cut on the inside or back a two-line inscription in Script and in Block. For the script inscription, usually an address, design small, neat letters. Design straighter and more angular appearing script, so that all cuts including hair-line connections can be made with as little curve as possible. This will eliminate turning of the block which is the main difficulty in cutting concave surfaces with a regular script graver. Gravers bent to overcome obstacles encountered on inside curved surfaces are not always obtainable so it is best to learn to do this with a straight graver.

Certain cuts like crossing the lower case "t" appear to be impossible, but are not, as a little practice will prove. Most experienced engravers rely on the script graver for all work. If the novice does not get results after much effort, and curved or bent gravers are not obtainable, then it becomes necessary to bend a straight graver to suit the surface. A regular script tool may be softened and bent in the desired shape. See Figs. 47 and 72A. This requires only two bends and care must be taken to keep the line of centers true. Draw the temper to a pale straw color. This graver is good only for the problem cuts and not adaptable to the regular diagonal cuts that can be done with a regular graver.

A special type of block letter is used for cutting on concave surfaces. It is an adaption from the Roman alphabet. Slant the letters about the same as the script work already explained. For all stems, use a single bright cut with a script graver. For the bars, which are all parallel with the edge of the bracelet, use a thin cut that will contrast with the bright cut stem. Serifs present a problem and may be put on with a single cut or pick, approaching the cut from the most logical direction. Due to the curve it will be found impossible to place some serifs as learned in Roman. The beginner must learn to improvise here in order to maintain the true form. For cutting a bracelet on the inside or back, clamp it directly in the open

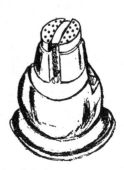

Fig. 73. Bracelet is held directly in jaws of the block.

jaws of the block in the same manner as illustrated in Fig. 73. The bracelet is, of course, in an inverted position.

For practice, cut two narrow strips of copper plate and soft-solder them together so that the result resembles a round child's bracelet. This furnishes an excellent surface for outside and inside work. On the outside, cut single names in script and block using a liner and flat graver. Mark off a few spaces large enough to hold three initials; design and cut these in script and block.

For inside cutting the curve will be found more severe and hence more practice is needed. First cut the script alphabet and numbers. Then try an inscription like this: "To Mary from Aunt Jean—1945." Again use an angular script design as the straighter cuts are simpler to execute and if done properly the effect is interesting and easily read.

Next, design and cut a similar block inscription with the same slanted style as used on the back of identification bracelets.

To hold the bracelets while cutting, they may be clamped in the open jaws of the block without using attachments. On actual bracelets, care should be taken not to mar the article. Chamois or flannel should be used to protect it.

To shape a surface simulating a loving cup, curve severely an entire copper plate. Loving cup inscriptions are sometimes large so use up as much space as possible, taking care only to keep the inscription centered. Lay out a four-line inscription similar to this:

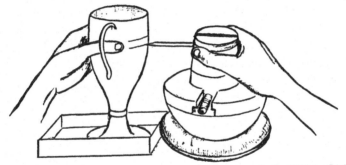

CLAMP MARKER IN BLOCK. TURN CUP WITH BASE NESTLED IN CORNER OF BOX. LINES WILL BE STRAIGHT.

Fig. 74. Lining off loving cup with marker held in block.

"Lions Award, won by James L. Heather, Jan. 21, 1949." On this inscription emphasize "Lions Award"; second emphasis is placed on "James L. Heather"; "won by" and "Jan. 21, 1949" will be designed the same size, that is, smaller than either of the other two lines. Use a large liner to wriggle the "Lions Award." Square off tips with tiny serifs. "James L. Heather" should be about half the size and a 38 flat graver will do nicely. The "won by" and "Jan. 21, 1949" can be cut with a 36 flat graver. Capped block or picked block can be used. Fig. 74 shows how a loving cup is marked off, using a marker clamped in the block.

Curve two plates in the same manner for baby cups. Baby cups usually have a single name to engrave. Sometimes the complete name and date of birth is added. Lay out in the center of the right side of the cup, a two-line inscription in script. The name line should be larger than the date line. The date line should fall closely under the name line as a wide gap spoils the appearance.

Fig. 75A shows how the baby cup is held in the jaws of the block while engraving. Chamois or flannel is used between the jaws and cup to prevent marring the surface, but in order to illustrate better the method of holding various articles the chamois or flannel is omitted in this and subsequent illustrations of this nature.

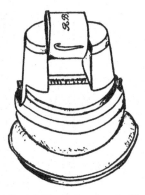

Here is an excellent surface on which to show your best work. Script is generally more desirable than block. Block with a liner presents a nice effect but should not be done with a wide tool. A flat tool can be used but better results are obtained with a liner. Lay out and cut the same type of inscription using liner and flat graver.

FIG. 75A. Baby cup held in block, ready for engraving.

Fig. 75B shows how baby cups are lined off quickly and accurately using a pegwood marker. The marker is useful for many other jobs and is constructed quite simply as shown in Fig. 75C.

FIG. 75B. Lining off baby cup with pegwood marker.

Curve two plates in the same manner. On one, design and cut a ribbon monogram about 1⅛ inches in diameter. This is often done on the outside of a deep bowl or pitcher. On the other plate, cut a cross-lined block monogram, diamond shaped, about one inch in width. This is also practical work for the outside of silver hollowware.

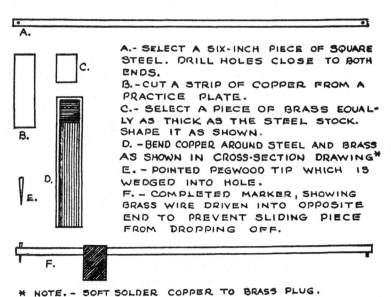

A.- SELECT A SIX-INCH PIECE OF SQUARE STEEL. DRILL HOLES CLOSE TO BOTH ENDS.

B.-CUT A STRIP OF COPPER FROM A PRACTICE PLATE.

C.- SELECT A PIECE OF BRASS EQUALLY AS THICK AS THE STEEL STOCK. SHAPE IT AS SHOWN.

D. –BEND COPPER AROUND STEEL AND BRASS AS SHOWN IN CROSS-SECTION DRAWING*

E. – POINTED PEGWOOD TIP WHICH IS WEDGED INTO HOLE.

F. – COMPLETED MARKER, SHOWING BRASS WIRE DRIVEN INTO OPPOSITE END TO PREVENT SLIDING PIECE FROM DROPPING OFF.

* NOTE.- SOFT SOLDER COPPER TO BRASS PLUG.

FIG. 75C. Construction of a simple marker.

Shape six pieces of metal to represent the backs of 16-size pocket-watches. To shape the copper, use a wooden dapping-block and punch (see Fig. 76) sold by jewelers' supply houses for removing dents from watch case lids. Use a 16-size punch, and a recess in the block that matches it. Place the copper plate between punch and die, and hammer the punch with a fairly heavy hammer or rawhide mallet. Three or four heavy blows should be sufficient as many light blows tend to wrinkle the edge of the cup. With metal-cutting hand-shears trim the surplus metal from the edges. Rough edges or burrs may be smoothed off by rubbing them over coarse emery paper.

Design and cut:

1. Three-letter Ribbon Monogram covering about 3/4 the space.
2. Three-letter round, Block Monogram using about 2/3 the space.
3. Three Roman letters, cross-lined and shaded, and off-shaded. These letters must not be oversized. They should be just large enough so that the stems are wide enough to fill-in nicely. Spacing between the letters should not be crowded and a cross-lined period should be used to match the letters.

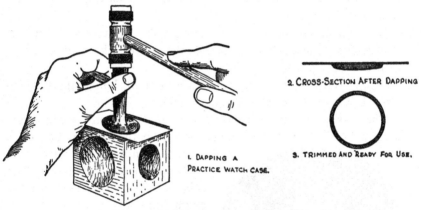

FIG. 76. Making practice watch backs.

4. A five-line Gothic inscription using small neat letters; cut with a round graver. (On outside.)
5. A five-line Script inscription, small neat letters. (On outside.)
6. A five-line Block inscription using No. 1 flat graver or No. 36 (depending on width of the graver). (On outside.)
7. A five-line Script inscription on the inside of the watch back. Considerable lift on the graver is needed here.
8. A five-line Block inscription on the inside using a No. 1 flat graver. Much lift is essential to clear the edge.

Casket plates are usually of a very soft metal and present no real cutting problem except in the size of the letters. In script cutting, the shade cuts are quite long and for this reason difficult to execute. A regular script graver may be used with the graver extended in the handle to make a longer tool. This is necessary to execute the exceptionally long cuts. Some engravers use a No. 49 flat graver for script and block work. The beginner may try both and make his own choice. The No. 49 flat graver is excellent for "squaring off" such as the top of the lower case "t." Usually a full name is wanted and it is centered in the same manner as on much smaller articles. If the dates are wanted, the birth date is located in the upper left corner. The date of death is located in the lower right hand corner.

Old English makes an outstanding job. Design as usual and wriggle-cut using a No. 42 or No. 44 flat graver. Shade prominently with a script graver.

Simple Block with a flat graver can be used, but Script and Old English are more suitable in appearance.

The casket plate may be engraved by placing it on the engraver's solid pad (Fig. 77). As curved cuts are made, the pad may be moved

or rotated in much the same manner as the engraver's block. The solid pad also serves as a base for engraving many other articles too large or too unhandy to be held by regular block attachments.

For inside ring engraving, cut narrow strips of copper in various ring widths and sizes. They can be

FIG. 77. Engravers' pad.

soldered with soft solder. Use a jeweler's ring mandril to shape them. Brass practice rings can also be made or purchased (Fig. 78). They will be firmer and steadier although the metal does not cut as smoothly as copper. Practice the simple Script alphabet and numerals inside until good results are seen. The ring can be held in the fingers, braced in a grooved piece of wood clamped in the block, or a ring clamp attachment can be used (Fig. 79). Considerable lift should be used and a short belly is desirable. Here again all cuts can be made with a straight graver. Bent gravers can be bought especially for this work and if the reader feels he can get better results with them, by all means use them. Some engravers find this work easier if they use

FIG. 78. Brass prac-
tice ring.

FIG. 79. Ring clamp
attachment.

a greater script slant, some prefer a lesser script slant. The slant used is not important if the work and the slant are consistent.

The block alphabet is especially adaptable here. Practice the slanted Roman alphabet (explained under Identification Bracelets).

FIG. 80. Signet ring is clamped
in block between pieces of soft
wood.

FIG. 81. Compact clamped
in block.

Use broad stems or shade lines so that letters may be easily read. Tips or serifs may be over-emphasized to strengthen the appearance. Use regular script numerals when doing inscriptions. Inscriptions usually read as follows: "G. F. E.—H. R. N. 9-21-38." "To" may be preferred instead of the dash, so use a small "to." The contrast is good with block initials. When doing script initials, you would naturally use script throughout.

In concluding item 1, it is well to consider how some other objects are clamped in the engraving block. Signet rings, usually having a flat surface for engraving, must be held firmly. See Fig. 80. Clamped between two pieces of soft wood, the ring cannot shift its position during cutting.

Fig. 81 shows how a compact is held for engraving. Remember, all articles must be held with flannel or chamois to prevent the attachments from marring the surfaces.

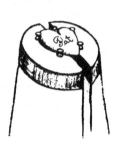   

Fig. 82. Locket in   Fig. 83. Tie clip in
pin attachments.   special holder.

Fig. 82 shows a locket held by pin attachments. Fig. 83 shows a small plate (detached from a tie clip) being held in the four-in-one attachments. Their use is so varied it should be considered money well spent to purchase a set.

2. Cementing Work

Cut out several pieces of copper, ankle bracelet size, and two pieces key-chain tag size. On the bracelet tags, cut single names in script, vertical script, block with flat graver, liner and round graver. Cut three initials in script, vertical script and block with flat graver and liner. On the key-chain tag, cut three drop Roman letters using only two periods centered between letters, or periods can be placed immediately following each letter in their usual position. The first treatment is more pleasing to the eye. On the other tag, cut three drop-script letters looping them together. These tags are usually too small to be held in the block attachments so it will be necessary to cement them on a plate and clamp the plate in the block. See Fig. 84. A plain brass plate will do very well and chasers' or engravers' cement can be used. Warm the plate over an alcohol flame and allow the cement to run slightly over the edges of the plate. Tags may be placed in the cement while it is cooling.

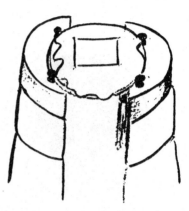

FIG. 84. Name tag is cemented to a plate to be held in engraver's block.

3. Transferring Designs

For practice cutting on silver flatware, cut 16 strips of copper in the general shape of a fork handle. Carefully design and cut near the top of the piece:

1. One Old English letter ribbon cut.
2. One slanted script letter.
3. Three vertical script drop letters.
4. One block monogram. This design should be narrow and long conforming with the shape of the piece to be engraved. A narrow liner should be used as a wide liner produces a bulky looking monogram.

When a job involves engraving many pieces with the same initial or monogram, like on the handles of knives, forks and spoons, the design can be printed or transferred from the first piece that has been cut, without repeating the labor of drawing it separately on each of the pieces.

For each design, make additional transfers, using the Buffalo pad (Fig. 85). To do this, fill-in cutting with powdered chalk. Press design on pad lightly and remove. The powder adheres to the pad and a clear design shows. Prepare a blank piece by smearing a thin film of transfer wax or beeswax on the surface. Place over impression on pad, lightly press and remove. A clear print will show in the wax. This may be cut as it is or traced with a steel point, wiped off and cut. Several prints can be made from one impression. There are many other ways to transfer designs but since none are better

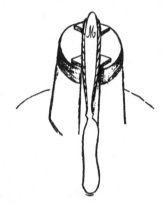

FIG. 85. Buffalo Transfer Pad.   FIG. 86. Flatware in special holder.

or quicker than the above method they will not be mentioned here. Fig. 86 shows how to hold flatware securely, using the grooved attachments.

4. Duplicating Signatures

Occasionally there is a call for transferring and cutting signatures on flat plates or fountain pens. The procedure is as follows: Have the person write the signature the desired size on a piece of paper. Rub pencil lead dust or lamp-black on the back of the paper. On the surface to be engraved, place a thick creamy coat of Chinese white. Place the paper in position and trace, with a hard pencil, the outline of the signature. A clear black line will appear on the article. Then cut, using a line of consistent width, no variation, such as a pencil or pen would make.

5. Designing and Cutting Emblems

Refer to Fig. 87 for the layout and design of six popular emblems. As the design is mainly mechanical (excepting the elks head in emblem 6) there is little to be said that the reader has not already learned in the section devoted to monograms.

The cutting is done using the script graver for all primary cuts such as outlining, shading, and most fill-in treatments. In emblems

1-MASONIC EMBLEM
2-ROTARY EMBLEM

3-KIWANIS EMBLEM
4-KNIGHTS OF COLUMBUS

5-LIONS EMBLEM
6-ELKS EMBLEM

Fig. 87. Design layout for six popular emblems.

2, 3, and 4 the lettering style is Gothic and indicates a round graver. The background of the large "L" in emblem 5 may be filled-in with matting (cross-wriggle with a liner) or close "picks" using a round graver. The background of the shield in emblem 4 may be treated in the same way. In the emblem 6, the Roman numerals may be cut with a small flat graver.

Select, design, and cut two of the illustrated emblems. The first may be designed 1¼ inches in diameter; the second, ¾ of an inch in diameter.

6. Cutting for Fill-in Work

On a piece of plastic or celluloid, design a ribbon monogram, three ribbon drop letters, and two block inscriptions. The block inscrip-

FIG. 88. Monofil.

tions should be the size adaptable for the barrel of a fountain pen; two lines, name and address, one cut with a flat graver, the other with a round graver. Cut the ribbon monogram with a script graver taking care not to cut too deep or edges will become fuzzy. Cut the drop letters with a script graver using a ribbon cut. Cut the block inscriptions as already described and fill in with Monofil (Fig. 88), which is sold by jewelers' supply dealers. This is applied by rubbing on until all cuts are filled. Then, remove surplus by rubbing with a crumpled piece of hand tissue paper. Any soft fiber paper will pull the Monofil out of the cuts.

7. Making Inscription Plates

Brass inscription plates are often cut and the engraving filled in black by applying antimony chloride solution, obtainable at any drug store. This is done by brushing the solution over the lettering and allowing it to dry. Then, line-finish the plate, removing all the black oxidation except in the cuts, using emery paper grit No. 0, rubbing the brass so as to produce a satiny-looking surface, made of parallel scratched lines. Wipe the plate clean with white cotton, and lacquer with medium-thin clear lacquer.

Brass is tough and offers more resistance than copper and silver. It is not brittle although some cast brass door knockers are flaky in cutting. The beginner's problem is to become adept at cutting the brass used in inscription plates, cigarette lighters, and the less expensive compacts and cigarette cases.

For practice work, select a plate the size of a regular copper practice plate. Line finish the plate using No. 2 emery paper. This may be done by laying the plate flat and wrapping a section of emery paper around a flat piece of wood about 3 inches wide and five inches long.

Design and cut a 4-line Roman inscription. This style is especially adapted to fill-in treatment, with antimony chloride solution.

The real secret in successfully cutting brass is in having a graver in perfect condition, no suggestion of a rounded edge. For an inscription plate of this nature very carefully select a graver with the proper lift. There must be no risk of slipping. Have the left side of the belly (belly view, looking at both sides) highly polished. Brass has a definite tendency to cut dull and rather rough unless great care is exercised. A sharp cutting edge with a highly polished belly will result in the maximum smoothness and brightness of cut that can be gotten from the metal. Care must also be taken to prevent the tool from "picking up" brass. Examine the tool after a few cuts and if the cutting edge shows a yellow color the graver is "picking up" brass and is a definite indication that the following cuts will be rough and dull unless the brass is polished away. This condition can also cause slips.

When the plate is cut, it can be line-finished lightly with No. 0 emery paper. Wipe off the plate with dry cotton or cleansing tissue; then, lacquer the plate using a flat camels hair brush and very thin lacquer. A brush ¾ of an inch wide will do very well. Apply quickly and allow the lacquer to smooth itself out. Continuous brushing will leave a streaked finish. It is always necessary to lacquer brass plates to prevent tarnishing. If black letters are desired, antimony chloride solution may be used as explained. This may also be lacquered in the same manner.

Select a brass plate half the size of a regular copper practice plate. Line finish with No. 2 emery paper until all blemishes disappear. Lay out a 3-line Gothic (block) inscription. Use a No. 52 round graver. Be sure the graver is in perfect condition; then, cut and finish plate in the same manner as on the Roman plate described in the preceding paragraphs. This style is very good when easy-to-read, simple letters are desired.

Select a brass plate the size of a copper practice plate. Prepare with emery as explained, lay out and cut a four-line script inscription. This cutting requires a bit of technique. Good script should always be positive in appearance but here the engraver must cut quite positively and definitely. Script cutting on brass is deeper than average script cutting on other metals. It will be found that delicate hair-lines are hard to achieve and fortunately are not much required. Remember, the final line-finishing will lighten all hair-line cutting and possibly obliterate those cut too lightly. Script on brass should be done prominently with wide shade lines and hair-lines that are wider and deeper than usual. If cut so, the work is equally attractive whether filled in black or left plain. If trouble is had obtaining a wide shade line, two cuts for each shade line may be used to good advantage.

On a practice brass plate, design and cut three horizontal ribbon letters interwoven. This style is especially adaptable to ladies' compacts and is much in demand. The compact usually has a light coat of lacquer, so to prepare a similar surface, line finish the brass plate and lacquer first. Allow to dry thoroughly before designing and cutting. Do not lacquer after cutting. This may seem odd because surely the cuts will tarnish in a short time. However, an engraver cannot be expected to remove the lacquer, engrave and relacquer every inexpensive compact that comes in for engraving. Compacts are of such a variety of odd shapes that it would be well-nigh impossible to turn out a smooth lacquer finish with the usual available equipment.

For final work on brass, design and cut initials that would be suitable for cigarette lighters and similar articles. Use Script and Roman; Block with a flat graver and round graver. Considerable practice is necessary before the beginner will feel sure of himself, so if the first attempts on brass are unsatisfactory and improvement is slow, the beginner must keep in mind that no one has an easy time with brass in the beginning. It is the slow process of continual experience with the metal that brings results. An experienced engraver shows no hesitancy about brass cutting.

8. Designing and Engraving Comprehensive Sample Plate

The student who has completed all instructions in designing and cutting is now ready to design and engrave a final plate. See Fig. 89 for a suggested layout.

A recommended size for a final plate is $5\frac{1}{2}''$ x $8''$. The plate should be considerably thicker than the smaller copper practice plates, obviously because the larger size would be subject to bending as it is handled.

For easier handling in the engraving block, the plate can be mounted on a board. A narrow strip of wood may be nailed to the underside so that it can be clamped firmly in the engraving block.

Since the raw sheet of copper may have rough or sharp edges, it would be well to bevel these edges on the top-side and smooth the sharp edges on the underside for safety in handling. Then, apply an excellent line-finish prior to engraving the plate. Carefully execute the line-finishing operation with the lines running parallel to the length of the plate.

After completing all the engraved designs on the final plate, the surface may be very lightly line- or satin-finished to remove minute scratches that occur during engraving. Do not overdo the operation, for excessive line-finishing would detract from the fine engraving which should show sharp cuts and delicate hairlines.

Carefully rub the plate with soft flannel or cotton (dampened with alcohol) to remove any greasy spots or discolorations. Then, using a clear, thin lacquer, apply quickly with a $1\frac{1}{2}''$ fine textured brush to avoid streaking; brushing in the direction of the line-finish.

The final plate can now be framed, if desired, and put on display. It can also be shown to a prospective employer as a sample of one's proficiency in the art of engraving.

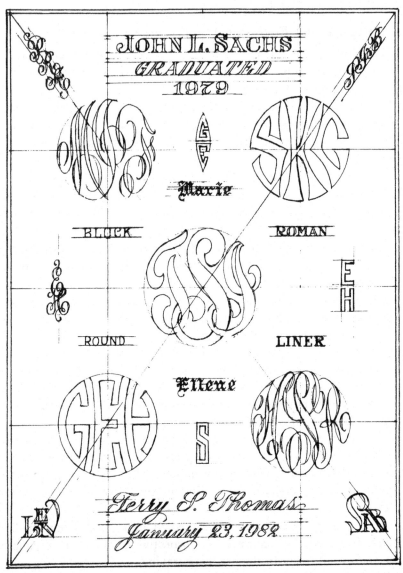

FIG. 89. Suggested lay-out for final plate.

Glossary of Engraving Terms

Among engravers, there are certain different terms used which may mean the same thing, and naturally would be confusing to a beginner. For instance, the terms "belly" and "heel" are identical in meaning. This Glossary is intended to avoid any misunderstandings that could arise from either duplicate or conflicting terms. Some of the terms the author believes are defined here for the first time in any publication.

Arkansas oil-stone: A natural white, smooth stone used for polishing gravers after grinding on India oil-stone.

Back-cut: A return cut over the same line as with a round graver in Gothic lettering.

Bars: The horizontal cuts or lines in block-letter designing.

Belly: The two bottom sides of the graver as illustrated in Figs. 8, 9, 10, under "Stoning Belly and Face."

Belly angle: Illustrated in Figs. 8, 9, 10, under "Stoning Belly and Face."

Blackstone: A popular modern alphabet resembling Old English.

Bright cut: A single cut of some width as a script shade cut or a cut done with a flat graver. Also, used to distinguish a cut made with a highly polished graver from that made with an unpolished graver.

Burnish: to remove a slip by using a burnisher.

Burnisher: A very hard piece of steel or stone, highly polished and placed in a handle. The most popular engravers' burnisher has a curved tip.

Capped block: Block letters in which the end of stems and bars are squared off with a "cap" similar to the Roman Serif.

Cipher: A script or ribbon monogram in which the letters are interwoven.

Columbia Text: A popular alphabet somewhat simpler in appearance than Old English.

Closelining: A ribbon-cut used particularly in ciphers, ribbon monograms and many artistic monograms.

Cross-lining: A popular type of fill-in used in all types of letters, relief work and monograms. It consists of closely cut parallel lines.

Cross-shading: Same as cross-lining.

Cross-wriggling: A type of fill-in used in relief work and in monograms. A liner is used by wriggling in vertical lines first, then wriggling horizontal lines directly over the vertical ones.

Diagonal drop-script letters: Script capital letters placed on a diagonal line.

Double-cut: See item 14 in Chapter 1.

Down-cut: Any cut downward in the direction of the base or horizontal line.

Drop connected block letters: Block initials connected vertically or diagonally.

Drop-script letters: Script capital letters placed on a vertical or diagonal line.

Dull cut: A cut made with an unpolished graver as compared to a bright cut.

Face: See "Graver Sharpening: Script Tool," Figs. 6 and 7.

Face angle: See Graver Sharpening: Script Tool," Fig. 6.

Fancy Block: Any decorative style of block or variation from the simple styles.

Fill-in: Used in relation to large letters that are done in outline and require a pattern cut within the outline.

Flowered letters or monograms: Block or ribbon letters with small flower designs in the main stems.

Gothic: See Fig. 63.

Heel: Same as "belly."

Hair-line: A cut of minimum width and depth executed with a script graver.

India oil-stone: A quick cutting stone made of grains of synthetic corundum, excellent for grinding hard steel.

Japanese lettering: Sometimes called Chinese lettering. A unique lettering design that resembles Japanese and Chinese figures.

Leaf letters: Any style of letters with ornamental leaf designs, usually worked into the main stems.

Leaf monograms: Any style of monogram with ornamental leaf designs worked into the stems.

Leonard Script: See Fig. 34.

Lift: See Fig. 10 under "Stoning Belly and Face."

Line finish: A smooth, dull-finish done with various grits of emery in which the parallel lines are clearly seen.

Lower case: The small letters of any alphabet as compared to the capital letters.

Matting: Same as cross-wriggling.

Mirror finish: The most brilliant polish obtainable on precious metals; gold and silver particularly.

Monogram: Two or three letters placed together in a pleasing and artistic arrangement.

Off-shading: A light cut or hair-line spaced away from the regular shade cut given fill-in letters.

Old English: See Fig. 65 for designed Old English alphabet.

Pearl Roman: An artistic variation of Roman, light and airy in appearance.

Pick: Term used to "square-off" a flat graver cut, or a script cut such as the top of a lower case "t."

Picked Block: Simple block style, "squared off" letters using picks.

Picking-up (metal): After making several cuts in copper or brass, a tan color may be noticed just under the cutting edge of the belly, of a trace of metal adhering to the steel of a graver. If not removed immediately, the following cutting will be rough and difficult.

Relief monogram: Monograms in which the background is filled in and the letters are not.

Ribbon: Used generally to refer to the Ribbon Alphabet. Also used to denote method of cutting.

Ribbon-cut: Term used to denote all cutting where more than two shade lines, placed close together as in regular ribbon cutting, are used.

Ribbon-shaded letters: Letters that are shaded with ribbon cuts.

Roman: A style of block cutting illustrated in Fig. 43.

Running initials: Used to denote three interwoven letters located on a horizontal plane.

Satin-finish. A polish with a satiny appearance. Not as bright as a mirror finish.

Script: See drawings in Fig. 30.

Script Slant: The correct slant for all script cutting as illustrated in Fig. 34.

Script tools: More correctly called script gravers. Many engravers refer to all their gravers as "tools."

Serif. See Fig. 44. The tips placed at the ends of stems and bars peculiar only to this alphabet.

Shade-cut: In Script, the wide cuts as compared to hair-lines. In Block, the cut used to shade a filled-in letter.

Shading: Generally used to refer to wide bright cuts or ribbon-cuts placed on filled-in block letters. Refers also to the wide cuts used to accent some ribbon monograms or ciphers.

Shadow-line letters: Same as cross-lined letters.

Signet ring: A ring with designated space for engraving on it, an initial, monogram or any other design. This space is located at the top-outside of the mounting.

Simplified script: See Fig. 30.

Single-shaded letters: Letters that are shaded with one bright cut.

Slanted block: Any block letters that are not vertical in construction. The slant may be to the left or right.

Slanted Old English: Any Old English letters that are not vertical in construction.

Solid cut: A single shade cut or any single cut such as would be made with a flat or round graver.

Spacing: Generally applied to the correct arrangement of letters in any given word. It also applies to the exact arrangement of words as in designing an inscription.

Square graver: Any graver made from a piece of steel of square cross-section, commonly called a script tool or graver.

Square-off: To make square the raw end of a cut by using a "pick."

Stems: Generally applied to the basic cut or fundamental part of any letter. In block, it refers to the vertical cut.

Stylus: A rubber marker with a steel point on one end.

Transfer wax: A mixture of beeswax and tallow used for transferring designs.

Up-cut: Refers to any cut made in an upward direction, away from the horizontal base line.

Vertical Script: See Fig. 42.

Wriggle-cut: See Fig. 62.

Questions and Answers

Most of the following questions and answers deal with engraving problems. However, it is advantageous for the engraver to have knowledge of certain facts concerning jewelry work; so, the questions are chosen to cover all that we feel the engraver should know.

---

1. **What cleaning agents are generally used in connection with jewelry?**
   Soap, ammonia, cyanide and water solution, and soda.
2. **Which one would you use to remove tarnish?**
   Cyanide.
3. **Which one would you use to brighten the appearance of the article?**
   Soda.
4. **Which one would you use to remove dirt or greasy film?**
   Ammonia.
5. **What is used to remove scale formed in hard soldering?**
   A pickle solution composed of sulphuric acid and water. In a heated solution the proportions should be nine parts water and one part sulphuric acid. In cold solution the proportions should be eight parts water and two parts sulphuric acid. The work is plunged into the pickle while still hot from soldering.
6. **Is tripoli a cutting or polishing agent?**
   Cutting, because the abrasive grains are coarse.
7. **Is rouge a cutting or polishing agent?**
   Polishing, because the "grain" is very fine.

8. Are the same buffs used for both?
No.

9. What combination of ingredients make a good cleansing solution for removing tripoli, rouge, and generally cleaning the article?
Soap, soda, and ammonia with water.

10. Will cyanide remove rouge or dirt?
No.

11. What should be done about scratches or marred surfaces existing on an article, before engraving?
In some instances, the engraving may completely cover and obliterate an imperfection. If not possible to do this, it is wise to call the customer's attention to the blemish to establish the fact that it occurred prior to engraving. If the article is a sale of your store and the customer has not discovered it, a slight scratch may be removed by careful burnishing and buffing. It is always advisable to acquaint the salesman or the customer (as the case may be) with the condition of the article in question.

12. Suppose you made a slight slip of your graver on a line-finished compact and were able to burnish it out successfully, what would you use to restore the line finish over the burnished spot?
Emery paper.

13. Suppose you made a slight slip on a satin-finished piece of sterling and burnished it successfully, what would you use to restore the satin finish?
Rub lightly with a common ink eraser.

14. Suppose you slipped on a mirror-finished piece of sterling or gold and burnished successfully, what would you use to restore the mirror-finish?
A soft buff with rouge.

15. Suppose you slipped on a lacquered brass plate or compact, what would you do?
Remove lacquer with denatured alcohol, burnish, refinish, and relacquer.

16. Suppose you slipped on a piece of sterling and could not bur-

nish; would you grind it off with a tripoli buff on polishing motor, and re-engrave?

Yes.

17. Suppose you slipped on a gold-plated article and could not burnish, would you give it the same treatment?

No. The plating would be removed and the article ruined.

18. Suppose you slipped on a gold-filled article and could not burnish; would you grind it off and re-engrave?

No; this would ruin the article, if cheap grade. Yes; if of high-grade filled stock with thick outer layer of gold.

19. Suppose you slipped on a silver-plated article; would you grind it off and re-engrave?

No. The article would be spoiled.

20. Suppose you slipped on a solid gold article and could not burnish; would you grind it off and re-engrave?

Yes.

21. Name eight metals on which you will probably have to engrave.

Aluminum, silver, copper, brass, platinum, gold, palladium and steel.

22. How does aluminum cut?

Very soft, cuts flaky and gritty.

23. How does silver cut?

Soft and smooth.

24. How does copper cut?

Medium and smooth.

25. How does nickel cut?

Fairly smooth, slightly gritty, tougher than copper.

26. How does gold cut?

Hard according to karat (the lower the karat, the harder); usually smooth.

27. How does brass cut?

Hard and tough.

28. How does steel cut?

Always too hard for good cutting. Some is less brittle, if well annealed.

29. How does palladium cut?
Not very smooth or bright.

30. How does platinum cut?
Smoother than palladium, not bright.

31. On cigarette lighters, what base metal is generally used? What plating?
Brass base; chrome, silver or gold plate.

32. On an average lady's compact, what metals are generally used?
Brass and sterling.

33. Are loving cups generally white or yellow?
Mostly white. A few are yellow.

34. Are they generally plated or solid?
Plated.

35. If plated in white metal, is lead or aluminum apt to be the base?
Lead alloy, or Britannia metal; soft metal.

36. If gold plated, what is the base usually?
Brass or nickel-silver; may be marked E.P.N.S. (electro-plated nickel-silver); hard metal.

37. Would you wriggle or bright cut a lead base?
Bright cut is better.

38. Would you wriggle or bright cut a brass base?
Wriggle.

39. Your graver slips; what is the probable trouble?
Rounded point. Broken belly line.

40. Your graver cuts rough. Why?
It is either picking up metal or it has a rough cutting edge.

41. What causes a graver to pick up metal on the right side of the belly?
A graver just sharpened sometimes picks up metal as it makes its first two of three cuts. After making a few practice cuts, the problem usually disappears. A dragging belly caused by incorrect lift will cause a "pick-up" of metal.

42. **Your graver cuts too deep. Why?**
   Face angle is too blunt or the tool has an inverted "V" belly.

43. **Your graver leaves a trail. Why?**
   A trail is a mark caused by the belly dragging at the very beginning of a cut. This is caused by an incorrect lift. An extremely low belly angle will cause the belly to leave a line or trail just as the point enters the metal. An extremely high lift or greatly increased belly angle may cause a similar result if the graver is too long. It is well to note that a high lift is more satisfactorily controlled when the graver is short.

44. **You cannot get a bright cut. Why?**
   Graver is not polished enough.

45. **Your graver won't hold a point. Why?**
   Too soft. It should be re-hardened and tempered.

46. **Your graver breaks points. Why?**
   The face angle may be more than 45 degrees which weakens the point. It could be too hard or too brittle. Therefore, the temper should be drawn to a light straw color.

47. **To draw the temper do you use a gas flame, an alcohol flame or a bunsen burner?**
   Any blue or smokeless flame.

48. **The correct engraver's eyeglass or loupe should be a 2″, 2½″, 3″, 3½″, 4″, 4½″ or 5″ loupe?**
   A 4″ loupe.

49. **How is aluminum ware bright cut?**
   Keep graver highly polished and dip in kerosene, alcohol or turpentine.

50. **Where do you start when engraving inside rings?**
   Start at the 14K mark, engraving to the right.

51. **How do you hold signet rings?**
   Use two pieces of soft lead bars, place ring between the bars and clamp in engraving block. Two blocks of wood could also be used.

52. **Where is it desirable to use a graver that is not highly polished?**

On highly polished surfaces and satin finished articles. It will prevent slipping and leaves a dull gray cut.

53. **How do you lay out the blocking-in lines on large articles like loving cups, pitchers, etc.**

Clamp rubber marker or pointed pegwood in engraving block. Fit the base of the loving cup or pitcher in the corner of a low sturdy box next to the block for steadiness. Turn the article while holding block stationary. See Fig. 74.

54. **How are these articles held for engraving?**

Lay them on the leather base that the block rests in. This is concave and holds the articles so that they may be easily turned while cutting. If the article is too large, place it in a box cushioned with tissue paper.

55. **How do you proceed with engraving the inside cap of a gold watch?**

First remove the hinge-pin by tapping a pin pusher with a light hammer. Remove cap; then use cement rather than block attachments to hold it. These caps are usually very thin, so care must be taken to support it well with cement to avoid denting. When engraved, the cement may be removed by melting, and then soaking it in denatured alcohol.

56. **Is cementing advisable for other work?**

Yes. Some small articles have peculiar shapes and cannot be held securely in an engraving block. Many articles are too small to be held firmly in any of the block attachments, so cement is the answer.

57. **What style of lettering is best for small gold knives?**

Block. The engraving space is usually long and narrow. Three neat drop letters cut with a liner squared with picks is suggested as the most satisfactory style.

58. **What style would be best for the backs of small pins, fraternity pins, etc.?**

Small neat block using round or flat graver. The joint and catch are high which creates a great difficulty in maneuvering the graver. Slanted block letters solve the problem by allowing cuts that are placed to avoid contact with the protruding joint or catch.

59. **What style is best to use on the backs of crosses?**
Block is ideal with small flat or round graver, easily read. Some customers may specify script and this is allowable provided the name isn't too long. More letters can be gotten on in block and they are more readable than very small script.

60. **What style is best on the front of lockets?**
Usually a very small space is reserved for engraving. A small vertical script letter usually fits in better and also matches the design on the article.

61. **What style is best on sterling identification bracelets?**
Block (Gothic) with a round graver. Sterling wears quickly and any shallow cutting graver is undesirable. Roman can be used, cut with deep prominent strokes.

62. **What style is best on gold-filled identification bracelets or any gold-filled bracelets?**
Roman, ribbon cut for men's bracelets. Script for ladies' bracelets.

63. **What style is best for napkin rings?**
Script is first choice. Good for boys or girls. Neat block cut with a liner is also good.

64. **What style is best for baby cups?**
Script for boys and girls. Block with a liner is good.

65. **What style is best for baby spoons and forks?**
Script first, liner second.

66. **What style is best on the back of a man's wrist watch when the inscription is unusually long.**
A small round block graver. The result is neat and easy to read. This is a good style to use on all lengthy watch back inscriptions.

67. **What is best to use on a man's wrist watch, three initials only?**
Small Roman letters, ribbon cut. Script, flat graver and liner are used but the Roman style is neatest and most outstanding.

This, of course, applies to gold-filled, 14 karat gold or other precious metals. Watches with stainless steel backs should be engraved with an engraving machine.

68. **What is the best to use on the back of a pocket watch when a monogram is not wanted?**
Three Roman letters, cross-lined and shaded.

69. **What is best to use on a small lady's watch of gold-filled, 14 karat, or other precious metal quality?**
Small script letters. Roman is also used.

70. **Can stainless steel or base metal watch cases be cut?**
Yes.

71. **How?**
Use a liner; make the cut but do not lift out of the metal. Back out leaving burr. Trim off burr from the side with a flat graver. Other gravers can be used with success but for the beginner, this method is safer. Experience is essential here. The machine is, of course, the most desirable and the easiest method of engraving on stainless steel and other difficult-to-cut base metals.

72. **Is Chinese white the best medium for designing?**
Not necessarily. A film of beeswax dusted with a little bag of powdered chalk or "whiting" works very well. White showcard paint can be used instead of Chinese white and is much cheaper.

73. **Is it necessary to steel-point all designing?**
No. Only those designs that may be rubbed off as cutting progresses. On inscription work, the steel point should certainly be used.

74. **How can a jerky line be avoided when using the steel point?**
Do not hold the point perpendicular to the work, but rather increase the slant of the stylus and the point will glide smoothly over the surface.

75. **What can be used to prevent block attachments from marring the article while it is being engraved?**
Chamois-leather or flannel should be used between clamps and article to prevent nicks and scars.

76. **How may a transfer be saved for future use?**

It is sometimes necessary to save a transfer and a permanent impression is made. To do this, use a thin piece of cardboard, postal card thickness. Dampen contact area slightly. Place over design and rub over the area with a burnisher. When lifted up, the design will stand out in relief. Place close to a flame to dry out. This sets the design more permanently so that it can be used many times. To use this type of transfer, it is pressed on the article, which has been prepared with a light film of transfer wax. A light but clear transfer is the result. With this system, good results can be obtained using Chinese white on the article and lamp black on the transfer card. Some engravers use red cosmetic rouge. The medium is of no consequence so long as a clear transfer is shown. Transfers on cards can be filed away for further use.

77. **In block cutting why are some first letters made larger on inscription work?**

For emphasis on important words and also to present a pleasing appearance.

78. **In placing a long inscription in a limited space, can anything be done about the lack of space between the words due to cramping them too closely?**

Yes. Nothing can be done to gain space, but the first letter in each word can be made larger. This makes the inscription easier to read and leaves no doubt as to where one word stops and another starts. This is adaptable to all Roman and plain block work.

79. **In the block alphabet, what size are the numerals in relation to the capital letters?**

The same size.

80. **In the script alphabet, what size are the numerals in relation to the capital letters?**

$\frac{2}{3}$ the size.

81. **In the Old English alphabet, what size are the numerals in relation to the capital letters?**

$\frac{2}{3}$ the size.

82. **Does the plain block alphabet have a lower case? Does Roman?**

Yes, but they are not generally used by engravers.

83. **To engrave the inside of a watch back, how can you get to the cuts when the letters are designed close to the curved edge?**

A graver with a sudden, extreme lift is necessary. This can be a script graver, flat graver or round graver. If script is used, a graver with a short belly and high lift must be used for the cuts. If a flat graver is used, it will be found that all cuts can be made from two directions and so the curved edge can be avoided. A round graver for Gothic lettering is very adaptable here although the cutting appears to be almost impossible due to the raised curved edge. A special tool may be prepared for this type of work. Select a small round graver (#50), heat and bend sharply near the tip until enough lift is gotten to clear the raised edge of the watch back. Re-harden and draw. Any curved letter can be cut with ease with this tool.

84. **How about napkin rings with raised edges; how can they be cut without marring the edges?**

Very much like the preceding answer. Extreme lifts are necessary on all tools for this sort of work.

85. **Is it safe to leave Chinese white on the article indefinitely?**

No. It has been found that if Chinese white is left on a highly polished surface for a period of time, the surface is dulled slightly and it is necessary to buff the article to restore the finish. This becomes especially unhandy when the article happens to be a deep bowl with a monogram to be engraved in the bottom. If properly used, Chinese white is not at all injurious. Just don't leave it on too long.

86. **What are some of the usual errors made by beginners on actual work?**

1. Foremost is marring the article. Many a fine job has been ruined by nicks made by block attachments. Even wrapping the article with flannel sometimes leaves marks if gripped too tightly. Be sure there are enough layers of flannel between attachments and article. A marred article is a sure sign of carelessness.

2. Speed is the next common error. Some engravers never really develop their true ability because of too much emphasis on speed and not enough on quality of work. For a beginner, speed is ruinous. Its results are poor lay-out, many slips and burnishes and finally a "botch" job. The way to gain speed is to slow down and work carefully. Speed will be gained as experience is added.

3. Cutting designs that are too large for the article. Remember that engraving is not supposed to completely cover the given surfaces. Depending on the job to be done, the result should be neat and crisp looking, easy to read.

4. Weak looking designs with a minimum of cutting. All lettering is meant to be read and should be strong or bold enough to look well in the given space. Choice of a thin flat graver or liner simply because it is easier to handle invariably produces a weak appearance. On monograms, choice of a quick wriggle fill-in because it is easiest to handle is usually disappointing. More-so to the engraver than to the customer. Use the fill-in that you are sure will look best regardless of time spent. Most customers are willing to pay well for a really finished piece of work.

5. Overworking a design. There is a tendency among some students to lavishly clutter up an otherwise good design with innumerable scrolls, loops, whirls and such. This is a bad practice as it is time-consuming, confusing to the customer and is not required at all. The trend today is for simple designs that can be read. And this is a challenge to any engraver because it demands more perfect work. With simpler designs to deal with, a slight error is easily seen.

87. **When transferring silverware from a furnished sample, should a poor design be improved?**

No. The design must be cut as it is. Any change would be obvious and displeasing to the customer who no doubt has many pieces already engraved with the original design.

88. **When transferring silverware, should you improve the cutting if the sample shows inferior workmanship?**

Yes. There is no excuse for poor cutting even when obliged to cut a poor design.

89. **What is the best procedure to follow when engraving a large set of sterling flatware?**

    Procedures usually depend on individuals. One of the simplest ways to begin is to design and cut one of each article thereby getting comparative sizes of each design proportionate. Then the whole set may be transferred from these patterns and cut. To relieve monotony, transferring and cutting all forks, then knives, spoons, etc., is just as good a practice. It should be noted here that speed is attained not through rapid designing and cutting but by following a systematic routine of getting the work done.

90. **What about the alphabets not shown in this book such as Columbia Text, Blackstone, Pearl Roman, etc.? How are they cut?**

    The purpose of this book has been primarily to teach the student the simple and most used alphabets and how to cut them correctly. If the beginner has a good understanding of the structure of the alphabets covered here, then these other alphabets will present no real problem. Careful examination of any other alphabet will show that its components are similar to those in Script, Vertical Script, Roman, Simple Block or Old English and the cutting will follow along the same lines. Blackstone, for instance, can be handled very much like Old English although its general appearance is quite different. Many fancy block alphabets are directly based on Roman construction.

91. **Can an engraver "get by" without mastering Script?**

    No. Script is by far the most important alphabet. There have been instances where an engraver never really mastered script and so was forced to use a form of block or Old English for all work. Since script is in such demand, an engraver of this nature is not "getting by" because of his script deficiency. Usually the trouble is not in being able to cut script but in a poor understanding of the design. Thorough study and application of the structure of all script letters invariably results in greatly improved work. Once understood the problem disappears.

92. **To become a good engraver is artistic originality absolutely necessary?**

No. It helps considerably, but is not essential. The largest part of an engraver's work is in doing inscriptions, etc., that are based on alphabetic letters designed long ago. Letter constructions follow certain rules and forms and it only remains to find out what they are. Skill in drawing or designing will come to any one through continued practice.

93. **In reference to transfers on silver flatware, what is the best way to center a design when using a piece of paper or thin cardboard as the original?**

Mark off a center line on the original design. Mark off a center line on the article. Place the original over the article and when the two center lines coincide, the design is correctly centered. The same procedure may be used for centering any transfer from paper to the article. Monograms may be transferred from the bottom of dishes in this manner, or from the sides of pitchers and bowls.

94. **What is a cipher?**

Two or three script letters looped together in an artistic manner, usually fitted into a circular design.

95. **How can a design be corrected or altered without redesigning the entire inscription or monogram as the case may be?**

Use a small camels hair brush to apply more Chinese white over the small area that is to be re-touched or corrected. If grease and powder are used, the same brush may be used to dust powder over the desired spot.

96. **Are short tools more easily controlled?**

Not necessarily. The engraver should have script tools of various lengths. For example short cuts, especially curved, are handled with greater ease if the tool is short. On the contrary, a long shade line requires a much longer tool to get the maximum leverage for the power demanded in such a cut.

97. **If a Buffalo pad is not obtainable, what can be used as a substitute?**

Printers ink—roll gelatine can be melted and molded in the desired form for transferring. This can be secured from any printing company. To prepare, place gelatine in a double boiler and heat until melted. Then, pour into a can or tin of the desired size; allow to cool and solidify. The gelatine can then be removed and cut into several perfectly round pieces.

98. **What does E.P.N.S. stand for?**

Electro-plate on nickel-silver. This may be found on many hollow-ware pieces. The metal does not cut as smoothly nor as bright as sterling silver.

99. **Is there a specified length of belly for all script gravers?**

No. The length of belly should vary with the type of cutting done. Short curved cuts are more successfully executed with a short belly to prevent it from dragging. Larger work can be executed with a longer belly. The length range should be from 1/16 to 3/16 of an inch, depending on the type of cutting. A belly longer than this has no advantage.

100. **Is solid gold a correct term to use in referring to 10K, 14K, or 18K gold?**

The term "solid gold" is used to distinguish any karat grade of gold from gold-filled or gold-plate; meaning that the entire article is made of gold of the designated karat, without layers of base metal.

101. **What does the term "gold-filled" mean?**

This designates a composite metal-stock used for jewelry, watch cases, etc., that comprises alternate layers of gold (outside) and base-metal inside. It economizes cost of producing goods, by reducing the weight of gold needed, by the amount of weight of base-metal used in manufacturing the gold-filled sheet, wire, or other forms of stock.

102. **What does "rolled-gold plate" mean?**

"Rolled-gold plate" is made in the same manner as "gold-filled," but the iayer of gold is thinner.

103. **What does "gold plate" mean?**

The depositing of gold upon a base-metal by electro-plating. In European cases, the amount of electro-plate is measured in "microns" as 10 microns, 20 microns, 30 microns, 40 microns. The engraver may then judge the thickness of gold with which he must deal.

104. What does gilding or "gilt" mean?

The depositing of a very thin film of gold on any metal, by electroplating, or other processes.

105. What is sterling silver?

Sterling silver contains .925 pure silver and .075 of other metals.

106. What is coin silver?

Coin silver contains .90 pure silver and .10 of other metals.

107. What is nickel silver?

An alloy often used as a base for silverplated ware, generally containing 65% copper, 18% zinc, and 18% nickel.

108. What is German silver?

The same as nickel silver.

109. What is "burnishing" and how is it done?

Burnishing in relation to engraving means the removing of slips or scratches incurred during the process of engraving. It is done by using a curved-tip burnisher which should have a highly polished tip. Slips are removed by rubbing in a circular manner, starting at the shallow end of the slip and working the metal toward the center of the slip or cut. In this manner a light cut may be obliterated completely and a deep cut rendered less noticeable. The article usually requires a slight buffing on the polishing lathe to restore an even finish.

110. How may engraved copper plates be blackened or oxidized?

By using liver of sulphur, obtainable at any drug store. Adding water, make a thick paste and apply directly over the cuts. Heat the plate over a flame until the liver of sulphur preparation has turned black. Then, line-finish the plate, thus removing the excess and leaving a smooth finish. Clean plate thoroughly by wiping with a clean, dry piece of cotton. Lacquer the plate, using a medium-thin solution of clear lacquer. The technique is explained in Chapter 9.

111. How may silver plates be blackened or oxidized?

Silver may be treated in the same manner as copper.

112. How may brass plates be oxidized?

Apply butter of antimony (antimony chloride solution) to the article and allow to dry.

Index

A CATALOG OF SELECTED
DOVER BOOKS
IN ALL FIELDS OF INTEREST

A CATALOG OF SELECTED DOVER
BOOKS IN ALL FIELDS OF INTEREST

100 BEST-LOVED POEMS, Edited by Philip Smith. "The Passionate Shepherd to His Love," "Shall I compare thee to a summer's day?" "Death, be not proud," "The Raven," "The Road Not Taken," plus works by Blake, Wordsworth, Byron, Shelley, Keats, many others. 96pp. 5 3/16 x 8 1/4. 0-486-28553-7

100 SMALL HOUSES OF THE THIRTIES, Brown-Blodgett Company. Exterior photographs and floor plans for 100 charming structures. Illustrations of models accompanied by descriptions of interiors, color schemes, closet space, and other amenities. 200 illustrations. 112pp. 8 3/8 x 11. 0-486-44131-8

1000 TURN-OF-THE-CENTURY HOUSES: With Illustrations and Floor Plans, Herbert C. Chivers. Reproduced from a rare edition, this showcase of homes ranges from cottages and bungalows to sprawling mansions. Each house is meticulously illustrated and accompanied by complete floor plans. 256pp. 9 3/8 x 12 1/4.

0-486-45596-3

101 GREAT AMERICAN POEMS, Edited by The American Poetry & Literacy Project. Rich treasury of verse from the 19th and 20th centuries includes works by Edgar Allan Poe, Robert Frost, Walt Whitman, Langston Hughes, Emily Dickinson, T. S. Eliot, other notables. 96pp. 5 3/16 x 8 1/4. 0-486-40158-8

101 GREAT SAMURAI PRINTS, Utagawa Kuniyoshi. Kuniyoshi was a master of the warrior woodblock print — and these 18th-century illustrations represent the pinnacle of his craft. Full-color portraits of renowned Japanese samurais pulse with movement, passion, and remarkably fine detail. 112pp. 8 3/8 x 11. 0-486-46523-3

ABC OF BALLET, Janet Grosser. Clearly worded, abundantly illustrated little guide defines basic ballet-related terms: arabesque, battement, pas de chat, relevé, sissonne, many others. Pronunciation guide included. Excellent primer. 48pp. 4 3/16 x 5 3/4.

0-486-40871-X

ACCESSORIES OF DRESS: An Illustrated Encyclopedia, Katherine Lester and Bess Viola Oerke. Illustrations of hats, veils, wigs, cravats, shawls, shoes, gloves, and other accessories enhance an engaging commentary that reveals the humor and charm of the many-sided story of accessorized apparel. 644 figures and 59 plates. 608pp. 6 1/8 x 9 1/4.

0-486-43378-1

ADVENTURES OF HUCKLEBERRY FINN, Mark Twain. Join Huck and Jim as their boyhood adventures along the Mississippi River lead them into a world of excitement, danger, and self-discovery. Humorous narrative, lyrical descriptions of the Mississippi valley, and memorable characters. 224pp. 5 3/16 x 8 1/4. 0-486-28061-6

ALICE STARMORE'S BOOK OF FAIR ISLE KNITTING, Alice Starmore. A noted designer from the region of Scotland's Fair Isle explores the history and techniques of this distinctive, stranded-color knitting style and provides copious illustrated instructions for 14 original knitwear designs. 208pp. 8 3/8 x 10 7/8. 0-486-47218-3

Browse over 9,000 books at www.doverpublications.com

CATALOG OF DOVER BOOKS

ALICE'S ADVENTURES IN WONDERLAND, Lewis Carroll. Beloved classic about a little girl lost in a topsy-turvy land and her encounters with the White Rabbit, March Hare, Mad Hatter, Cheshire Cat, and other delightfully improbable characters. 42 illustrations by Sir John Tenniel. 96pp. 5³⁄₁₆ x 8¼.   0-486-27543-4

AMERICA'S LIGHTHOUSES: An Illustrated History, Francis Ross Holland. Profusely illustrated fact-filled survey of American lighthouses since 1716. Over 200 stations — East, Gulf, and West coasts, Great Lakes, Hawaii, Alaska, Puerto Rico, the Virgin Islands, and the Mississippi and St. Lawrence Rivers. 240pp. 8 x 10¾.

0-486-25576-X

AN ENCYCLOPEDIA OF THE VIOLIN, Alberto Bachmann. Translated by Frederick H. Martens. Introduction by Eugene Ysaye. First published in 1925, this renowned reference remains unsurpassed as a source of essential information, from construction and evolution to repertoire and technique. Includes a glossary and 73 illustrations. 496pp. 6⅛ x 9¼.   0-486-46618-3

ANIMALS: 1,419 Copyright-Free Illustrations of Mammals, Birds, Fish, Insects, etc., Selected by Jim Harter. Selected for its visual impact and ease of use, this outstanding collection of wood engravings presents over 1,000 species of animals in extremely lifelike poses. Includes mammals, birds, reptiles, amphibians, fish, insects, and other invertebrates. 284pp. 9 x 12.   0-486-23766-4

THE ANNALS, Tacitus. Translated by Alfred John Church and William Jackson Brodribb. This vital chronicle of Imperial Rome, written by the era's great historian, spans A.D. 14-68 and paints incisive psychological portraits of major figures, from Tiberius to Nero. 416pp. 5³⁄₁₆ x 8¼.   0-486-45236-0

ANTIGONE, Sophocles. Filled with passionate speeches and sensitive probing of moral and philosophical issues, this powerful and often-performed Greek drama reveals the grim fate that befalls the children of Oedipus. Footnotes. 64pp. 5³⁄₁₆ x 8 ¼.   0-486-27804-2

ART DECO DECORATIVE PATTERNS IN FULL COLOR, Christian Stoll. Reprinted from a rare 1910 portfolio, 160 sensuous and exotic images depict a breathtaking array of florals, geometrics, and abstracts — all elegant in their stark simplicity. 64pp. 8⅜ x 11.   0-486-44862-2

THE ARTHUR RACKHAM TREASURY: 86 Full-Color Illustrations, Arthur Rackham. Selected and Edited by Jeff A. Menges. A stunning treasury of 86 full-page plates span the famed English artist's career, from *Rip Van Winkle* (1905) to masterworks such as *Undine, A Midsummer Night's Dream,* and *Wind in the Willows* (1939). 96pp. 8⅜ x 11.

0-486-44685-9

THE AUTHENTIC GILBERT & SULLIVAN SONGBOOK, W. S. Gilbert and A. S. Sullivan. The most comprehensive collection available, this songbook includes selections from every one of Gilbert and Sullivan's light operas. Ninety-two numbers are presented uncut and unedited, and in their original keys. 410pp. 9 x 12.

0-486-23482-7

THE AWAKENING, Kate Chopin. First published in 1899, this controversial novel of a New Orleans wife's search for love outside a stifling marriage shocked readers. Today, it remains a first-rate narrative with superb characterization. New introductory Note. 128pp. 5³⁄₁₆ x 8¼.   0-486-27786-0

BASIC DRAWING, Louis Priscilla. Beginning with perspective, this commonsense manual progresses to the figure in movement, light and shade, anatomy, drapery, composition, trees and landscape, and outdoor sketching. Black-and-white illustrations throughout. 128pp. 8⅜ x 11.   0-486-45815-6

Browse over 9,000 books at www.doverpublications.com

THE BATTLES THAT CHANGED HISTORY, Fletcher Pratt. Historian profiles 16 crucial conflicts, ancient to modern, that changed the course of Western civilization. Gripping accounts of battles led by Alexander the Great, Joan of Arc, Ulysses S. Grant, other commanders. 27 maps. 352pp. 5⅜ x 8½. 0-486-41129-X

BEETHOVEN'S LETTERS, Ludwig van Beethoven. Edited by Dr. A. C. Kalischer. Features 457 letters to fellow musicians, friends, greats, patrons, and literary men. Reveals musical thoughts, quirks of personality, insights, and daily events. Includes 15 plates. 410pp. 5⅜ x 8½. 0-486-22769-3

BERNICE BOBS HER HAIR AND OTHER STORIES, F. Scott Fitzgerald. This brilliant anthology includes 6 of Fitzgerald's most popular stories: "The Diamond as Big as the Ritz," the title tale, "The Offshore Pirate," "The Ice Palace," "The Jelly Bean," and "May Day." 176pp. 5⅜ x 8½. 0-486-47049-0

BESLER'S BOOK OF FLOWERS AND PLANTS: 73 Full-Color Plates from Hortus Eystettensis, 1613, Basilius Besler. Here is a selection of magnificent plates from the *Hortus Eystettensis,* which vividly illustrated and identified the plants, flowers, and trees that thrived in the legendary German garden at Eichstätt. 80pp. 8⅜ x 11.

0-486-46005-3

THE BOOK OF KELLS, Edited by Blanche Cirker. Painstakingly reproduced from a rare facsimile edition, this volume contains full-page decorations, portraits, illustrations, plus a sampling of textual leaves with exquisite calligraphy and ornamentation. 32 full-color illustrations. 32pp. 9⅜ x 12¼. 0-486-24345-1

THE BOOK OF THE CROSSBOW: With an Additional Section on Catapults and Other Siege Engines, Ralph Payne-Gallwey. Fascinating study traces history and use of crossbow as military and sporting weapon, from Middle Ages to modern times. Also covers related weapons: balistas, catapults, Turkish bows, more. Over 240 illustrations. 400pp. 7¼ x 10⅛. 0-486-28720-3

THE BUNGALOW BOOK: Floor Plans and Photos of 112 Houses, 1910, Henry L. Wilson. Here are 112 of the most popular and economic blueprints of the early 20th century — plus an illustration or photograph of each completed house. A wonderful time capsule that still offers a wealth of valuable insights. 160pp. 8⅜ x 11.

0-486-45104-6

THE CALL OF THE WILD, Jack London. A classic novel of adventure, drawn from London's own experiences as a Klondike adventurer, relating the story of a heroic dog caught in the brutal life of the Alaska Gold Rush. Note. 64pp. 5³⁄₁₆ x 8¼.

0-486-26472-6

CANDIDE, Voltaire. Edited by Francois-Marie Arouet. One of the world's great satires since its first publication in 1759. Witty, caustic skewering of romance, science, philosophy, religion, government — nearly all human ideals and institutions. 112pp. 5³⁄₁₆ x 8¼. 0-486-26689-3

CELEBRATED IN THEIR TIME: Photographic Portraits from the George Grantham Bain Collection, Edited by Amy Pastan. With an Introduction by Michael Carlebach. Remarkable portrait gallery features 112 rare images of Albert Einstein, Charlie Chaplin, the Wright Brothers, Henry Ford, and other luminaries from the worlds of politics, art, entertainment, and industry. 128pp. 8⅜ x 11. 0-486-46754-6

CHARIOTS FOR APOLLO: The NASA History of Manned Lunar Spacecraft to 1969, Courtney G. Brooks, James M. Grimwood, and Loyd S. Swenson, Jr. This illustrated history by a trio of experts is the definitive reference on the Apollo spacecraft and lunar modules. It traces the vehicles' design, development, and operation in space. More than 100 photographs and illustrations. 576pp. 6¾ x 9¼. 0-486-46756-2

Browse over 9,000 books at www.doverpublications.com

A CHRISTMAS CAROL, Charles Dickens. This engrossing tale relates Ebenezer Scrooge's ghostly journeys through Christmases past, present, and future and his ultimate transformation from a harsh and grasping old miser to a charitable and compassionate human being. 80pp. 5³⁄₁₆ x 8¼. 0-486-26865-9

COMMON SENSE, Thomas Paine. First published in January of 1776, this highly influential landmark document clearly and persuasively argued for American separation from Great Britain and paved the way for the Declaration of Independence. 64pp. 5³⁄₁₆ x 8¼. 0-486-29602-4

THE COMPLETE SHORT STORIES OF OSCAR WILDE, Oscar Wilde. Complete texts of "The Happy Prince and Other Tales," "A House of Pomegranates," "Lord Arthur Savile's Crime and Other Stories," "Poems in Prose," and "The Portrait of Mr. W. H." 208pp. 5³⁄₁₆ x 8¼. 0-486-45216-6

COMPLETE SONNETS, William Shakespeare. Over 150 exquisite poems deal with love, friendship, the tyranny of time, beauty's evanescence, death, and other themes in language of remarkable power, precision, and beauty. Glossary of archaic terms. 80pp. 5³⁄₁₆ x 8¼. 0-486-26686-9

THE COUNT OF MONTE CRISTO: Abridged Edition, Alexandre Dumas. Falsely accused of treason, Edmond Dantès is imprisoned in the bleak Chateau d'If. After a hair-raising escape, he launches an elaborate plot to extract a bitter revenge against those who betrayed him. 448pp. 5³⁄₁₆ x 8¼. 0-486-45643-9

CRAFTSMAN BUNGALOWS: Designs from the Pacific Northwest, Yoho & Merritt. This reprint of a rare catalog, showcasing the charming simplicity and cozy style of Craftsman bungalows, is filled with photos of completed homes, plus floor plans and estimated costs. An indispensable resource for architects, historians, and illustrators. 112pp. 10 x 7. 0-486-46875-5

CRAFTSMAN BUNGALOWS: 59 Homes from "The Craftsman," Edited by Gustav Stickley. Best and most attractive designs from Arts and Crafts Movement publication — 1903–1916 — includes sketches, photographs of homes, floor plans, descriptive text. 128pp. 8¼ x 11. 0-486-25829-7

CRIME AND PUNISHMENT, Fyodor Dostoyevsky. Translated by Constance Garnett. Supreme masterpiece tells the story of Raskolnikov, a student tormented by his own thoughts after he murders an old woman. Overwhelmed by guilt and terror, he confesses and goes to prison. 480pp. 5³⁄₁₆ x 8¼. 0-486-41587-2

THE DECLARATION OF INDEPENDENCE AND OTHER GREAT DOCUMENTS OF AMERICAN HISTORY: 1775-1865, Edited by John Grafton. Thirteen compelling and influential documents: Henry's "Give Me Liberty or Give Me Death," Declaration of Independence, The Constitution, Washington's First Inaugural Address, The Monroe Doctrine, The Emancipation Proclamation, Gettysburg Address, more. 64pp. 5³⁄₁₆ x 8¼. 0-486-41124-9

THE DESERT AND THE SOWN: Travels in Palestine and Syria, Gertrude Bell. "The female Lawrence of Arabia," Gertrude Bell wrote captivating, perceptive accounts of her travels in the Middle East. This intriguing narrative, accompanied by 160 photos, traces her 1905 sojourn in Lebanon, Syria, and Palestine. 368pp. 5⅜ x 8½. 0-486-46876-3

A DOLL'S HOUSE, Henrik Ibsen. Ibsen's best-known play displays his genius for realistic prose drama. An expression of women's rights, the play climaxes when the central character, Nora, rejects a smothering marriage and life in "a doll's house." 80pp. 5³⁄₁₆ x 8¼. 0-486-27062-9